**CAPE POETRY PAPERBACKS**

Jeremy Reed
# ENGAGING FORM

Jeremy Reed

# ENGAGING FORM

JONATHAN CAPE
THIRTY-TWO BEDFORD SQUARE
LONDON

First published 1988
Copyright © 1988 by Jeremy Reed
Jonathan Cape Ltd, 32 Bedford Square, London WC1B 3EL

A CIP catalogue record for this book
is available from the British Library

ISBN 0-224-02574-0

Typeset by
Computape (Pickering) Ltd, North Yorkshire
Printed in Great Britain by
Biddles Ltd, Guildford and King's Lynn

for Pascale

Acknowledgments are due to the editors of the following magazines in which some of these poems first appeared: *Temenos, Literary Review, Poetry Book Society Supplement 1986, Strawberry Vale, Yale Review, Argos, Fiction Magazine.*

'Elegy for Senta' and 'Border Pass' were originally published as booklets by The Enitharmon Press.

'Bird Painter' and 'Floyd's Package' were hand-printed by Giles Leaman and published as respective booklets.

# Contents

# III

I

# Going

At Hill Farm, a downslope spread
   of creeping thistles untamed by a hoe,
a colony well rooted, cows would tread

a cluster flat in the meadow,
   but leave no gap that root buds wouldn't close.
A purple spike of plumes, a finch would show

a flash of pink, yellow or black
   alighting in a fixtured coronet.
Another field showed thistles in a stack,

rooted out, spiny for a fire,
   prickly as holly, more gregarious.
Two or three cows gaped over the barbed wire

of a field fence, that amber day
   I found the pappi silvering, white-haired
patriarchs, it was the still had them stay,

a puff of breeze, and they would fly,
   downy parachutes, light as gossamer,
luminous seeds snow-blown across the sky.

I stayed on, a glitter shook free,
   the air was squadroned with their drifting heads,
featherish stars flaking an alder tree.

I watched their going, a blizzard
   misting the valley, their random touch-down
would colonize fallow, hedgerow or yard,

their uplift varied with the wind,
   some had blown over the hill ridge and left
clusters of headless thistle stalks behind.

# Being There

Blue volutes sparkle in the tremolo
of water, looking out from a grotto

gouged by the tides, I watch the green and blue
of liquid jades resolve a single hue,

luminescent, striped, ruched into a skein
of coloured threads, each current holds a rein,

now slack in eddies, taut in the fast run:
the bay turns silver in the noonday sun . . .

I try to adjust to my being here,
a time-flash, film-still, a fuzz on the clear

shallows, that won't come right and rectify
the division felt between thought and eye,

my past lies unconfirmed by each new face,
sun-trapping, heads tilted back in a place

I knew as an extension of myself,
amethyst seaweed clinging to a shelf,

quartz sparkles veined in granite, a red can
on a rock-summit, bright as a mail-van.

I look again, the coast predicts no change,
the petals of the water rearrange

themselves, to a mauve iris tongued with blue.
It's not the place, it's I who can't renew

my sense of belonging, too close, too far,
at noon in a clear well, a vibrant star

is brighter than the sun. The water's cold.
My chin is cupped by a fine disc of gold.

# Marbles

Cool to the hand, an early memory:
our parquet floor made for fluidity –

a polished surface on which we'd compete
for coloured marbles in our stockinged feet,

the chalky, opalescent whites, a twist
of scarlet in crystal an adept wrist

would release for the strike, a navy blue
chipped from long service, its unusual hue

lent to it a prestige, an old warhorse,
stabled, unleashed only on the right course,

pocketed, coveted, and lodged inside
a velvet bag; we played against a tide

of domestic complaint, our galaxy
of coloured suns held its ascendancy

over the court of adults, meteorites,
explosive supernovas, stars in flight,

prismatic twinklings, the imagined spark
as a tiger's eye hummed to find its mark

in a green whorl intersected by pink,
the impact had it teeter on the brink

of the skyline, ricochet from the flash
before disorbiting in a weird dash . . .

Our games created war amongst the stars,
the cratered minerals, diamond-rayed pulsars,

little moon maps, or multicoloured eyes,
shifting their place in the unstable skies.

# Blockages

The light is on the inside of the trees,
   goldleaf that handpaints undersides,
and where I stand the stream is muddied lees,

choked by nettle, brooklime, great yellow cress,
   the black-gold nuggets of its bed –
exposures that the current cannot dress

with silken eddies; the flow's at a halt;
   a puling comes from the valley.
Words too, skirt edges of a fault,

the lines advanced so far, then like a horse
   grown nervous of an obstacle,
stopped in mid-flight before diverting course,

forked branchings, tributaries, a gapped split,
   the clear way through had disappeared,
the forceful line of issue seemed to hit

an invisible barrier, and slow
   to a cavalcade rucked in mud,
no lessening of ties could start that flow,

the retreat had been sounded. I came here,
   hoping to decongest the jam,
but found a muddied trickle, not the clear

incisive race of water, and went back;
   the hive turned silent in my head,
the stream a tie's width in the seasonal slack.

# My Father's Models

Glue from the wing-struts of a Tiger Moth;
you worked with a watchmaker's precision
at assembling models ostensibly
for my edification – it was yours,

the pleasure in the delayed completion,
the last coat of paint – I still remember
how you contrived to fashion a Junker
from metal splinters of a crashed aircraft

that shriekingly nosedived into the dunes.
These models were realities for you,
impractical exhibits I could touch,
but never use. They had become a craft

you practised in unsociably late hours,
leaving the varnished exhibit for me
to discover assembled on its mount,
the whisky vaporized in the decanter . . .

Mostly estrangement, our divergent lives
went wide of a pretended harmony,
and once seeing my father in the street,
and out of context, I could only run

for fear it wasn't him nose up against
a shop window. It's his face I recall
superimposed on mine in the mirror,
directing my shaving hand, a blood fleck

like a red eye in a white carnation.
Dark moods, I'd stay down in a sea-hollow,
only to be found out. Who was that man
made me return, instinctively follow?

Today at an airport, I find myself
recollecting planes to the last detail;
the one I broke, tried to conceal, and found
to my relief, restored, with a new tail.

# Bugging

Flotillas of mobile algae
   jerkily rotate in this pond,
cellular units too small for the eye,
   spherical, globular, concealed by frond –
whip-like flagellums, swimming hairs, they cross
      an oval pool the green of moss.

Survivors named from Greek legend,
   one-eyed, multi-armed, they compose
a tableau of monsters, features that lend
   a meaning to anatomies that rose
out of a fabled cave or marsh, tiny
      organisms, the water flea's

cyclopean eye, feelered head,
   the somersaulting hydra's tree
of tentacles, the water-bear, the red
   projectile of the stick-insect's body,
these are the erinyes that police the maze
      of a weed forest's sluggish haze.

The pond-skater on the surface
   rows leisurely, while on its back
the water boatman's listening to trace
   the vibrational pitch of fry and track
the source to an extinction – a black-out
      eclipses the newly hatched trout.

Nothing's safe in this bug empire,
   the diving beetle's torpedo
is no match for the tadpole; the red fire
   of a newt blazes from blue-indigo.
Then quiet, shadows like a panther's skin,
      deepen, as the thunder slams in.

# Sea Urchins

You cut your finger on that spiny shell,
  a still-life preserved exhibit
of a conchologist, a prickly pod,
a little apricot hedgehog,
  placed by thorny oysters, the bell
of a lilac top-shell. It was the drop
  of beady blood that wouldn't stop,
had you remember it.

Intrigued, you read of its anatomy,
  its heart-shaped test of limy plate,
the Aristotle's lantern of its gut
mottled with blues and purples,
  and how for its mobility
it circulates water inside, and moves
  by placing tube-feet in rock grooves,
an almost supine state.

And later found them beached on the strandline,
  brittle lampshades of brown or green,
the spongy mollusc eaten, the spines gone,
an annular sea-potato,
  washed clean by the ocean, saline,
smelling of the Atlantic. Or under
  weed, safe from the surf's thunder,
found one with the pristine

elemental glow of its pigment locked
  hard on the side of a rock-pool,
an obstinate unmoveable suction,
wedged tight and intractable.
  I looked on, complacent, unshocked,
this time, my fingers held in abeyance,
  their tips making the water dance
into my hands and cool.

# Mite

(magnified 1,600 times)

A horny crustacean, a blue lobster,
this one's individualized, tuskily
elephantine, on a pine needle squats,
its foot projections settle in like hooves
adaptable to variables of ground,
it swings the feelers of an octopus
in tactile browsings, when it shifts around
its congestion's an assembled army,
five thousand squatting by the sandy globe
of a rabbit's dropping –
                                    most burrow down,
or travel with the bee, a parasite,
blind to its host's itinerary.

In the blue light, the bristling antennae
of a springtail has picked up on its predator,
the mite flips it over and works to kill
with the tenacity of a spider,
its shell is almost jewel-like in combat,
the colour of a tiger's eye, glossy.

I look again, the cumbersome ritual
of two mating in a blue desert glare,
resembles moon-vehicles discarded
in a lunar quarry – the one piled high
on the other – the astronauts have gone.
A third intrudes, prawn-like, huge whiskerings,
the tusked legs trundling, withheld by the mass;
the beetle's ink-drop quivers in the grass.

# Perverse

A white chrysanthemum pinned in black hair,
a Japanese girl bends to a lily's
fluted champagne glass and inhales the scent
from its pink speckled throat. The garden chair's
canoed with scarlet leaves; Indian summer's
a mauve smoky plume – everything is still.
Her companion sits reading; a blackbird
is down, listening intently on the lawn.
The tension in still-life is evident,
twigs crackle as a substitute for speech.
Unpinning the flower she goes inside,
her quick step dances. He stays on reading,
thwarting her expectations, polishing
the red and yellow skin-down of a peach.

# Dragonflies

The water boatman backfloats on its beam,
a lazy coracle working the stream,

it listens for the vibration of fry.
Kidney-shaped rafts of frogbit pack an eye

around the pond's black pupil. Now I see
through the heat-shimmer the translucency

of wings defined by bluish-golden-green
scintillae grained into a turquoise sheen,

the hairclip body and thyroidic eyes
discernible from the traffic of flies

by its absorption into air. Its tack
is like a train engine's, forward or back

without turning, its aerial mastery
is hawk-sharp, a streamlined cruise, they flick free

in pursuit of a butterfly and land
it like a boarding party; reefed on sand

its white sails tear, it is flotsam adrift
on the face of the waters. Now I shift

my vision, at dusk the pond's a smudge-fire
of swarming insects, gnats that never tire,

midges thrown in the air like a fountain,
greendrake mayflies spilling out of the rain . . .

Two dragonflies are hunting, when they show
it is their kingfisher and violet glow

pronounces their flight pattern, a quick flit
assuring an imperceptible hit.

# Pond Skaters

Tension transmits a buzz to the surface,
duckweed flotillas buoy where a fine lace

of insects microdot the clear shallows.
A reed casts the imprint of a gallows

over a water-measurer's galley,
bridge-struts paralleling its nibbed body;

the whirligig beetle's circular spin
describes the dance of filings to a pin,

but it's the pond skaters' inverse shadows
filmed on the still skeins of the undertow,

in black clusters of spots, engage the eye,
before one sees them resting on the sky

reflected in the water's lens. They wait
for flies to tumble into the surfeit

of surface-drift – look: this one's light body
is upheld by the water's buoyancy,

the bristle-pads on its legs move so quick
across a plane of glass, each dimpled flick

is cushioned like a hoof on springy soil.
It retrieves a fly out of the blue oil,

its lifeguard's grip creates a stranglehold
on a victim that crackles, green and gold,

a pyre of shimmer – and is rowed behind
an island of frond, a green slatted blind

runs with a wind-glance, and a midge shower
dance as the light rays form a sunflower.

# Beechy Wood

A russet beechwood minting gold on red,
a squirrel's dash kicks up a trail of sparks –
leaves floating to a pheasant's tail.

I stand in light that coppers as it falls,
blue-grey capped oyster mushrooms periscope
like spore of a space colony
acclimatizing here, the mottled browns
of horn of plenty are polyparies
feeding on the tide-stream,
orange chanterelle, hedgehog-fungus,
each startles by peculiarities . . .

I move towards an awareness of change,
last year's leaves are still visible, the new
fall spangles an older decay.
A crow picks through leaf-litter, a blue jay
contests a magpie's rattle . . .

Silently I wait for beginnings, assimilate
beech-bark and leaf, become unobtrusive,
and see the flicker of a redstart's tail
stand up a moment like an orange sail.

# Lacunae

A Chinese-puzzle – even a decade
outdates one, and a new architecture
establishes a house built on a house,
the shell superimposed on in the way
a tooth's reinforced by a crown.
I poke sticks into a yellow fire's rage,
but claim no residue of ash.
History dies in that brief flash.

The mind grows troubled with amnesia,
each generation buries its forebears,
ten years consolidates no stance
of surety from which to advance?
Treading on so fragile a crust
each footstep leaves a powder-trail of dust . . .

The scarlet heart-shaped motif on her jeans
demands immediate appraisal. The girl
lives through her last day of being twenty,
already conscious of the gap
opening behind her. Then years in a day,
and growing old no one claims the same map,
or owns to being a contemporary.

# Fox Country

That summer, heat stretched our house on the rack,
the flaking timbers disjointedly baked,
the paint was splinters to the peppered grain
and pinkish undercoat.
Freelancing you bagged a gingerish stoat,
and ants packed into the raspberry stain
discolouring behind its head.
That fuse of volatile atoms lay dead,
bleached by the sun, byzantined by green flies.

Only our well remained a source of cool,
crystalline water come out of the hills,
it was our life-source, a white sickle moon
scarring the liquid membrane on that night
we drew silver from its circular pool,
a blade glinting in water.

At night, we read the edgy countryside,
contoured by pitch woods, it became a book,
a diagram corresponding to how
we saw it, a nocturnal alphabet
of tree-signs, spotting insects, the grammar
of owl and cricket; windows open wide.

We left before the rain seasoned the warp
of timbers – dry fire crackled in our blood,
a fox was running away from the sun,
red as the bracken outskirting a wood.

# Gravity

The earth we trust in, my right footstep leads
improbably across a fragile crust,
brittle as thaw-ice, a frosty egg-shell,
tested by machines, not the dinosaur's
boulder-shaped claw-prints in warm mud. I walk
the clock-hand round the global spin,
a fluttery pulse on the worn drum-skin
whose core is fire. Obedient to gravity,
we stay the hour; the dandelion has turned
fractionally sunwards on its stalk.

# Ivy

Is inevictable, its stranglehold
will uproot mortar from a wall, its stay
is untouched by the seasons, a fishnet
of green lockets placed like greaves on a tree

it's stunted by its gloss of arrowheads.
Battening where it goes, ivy ensnares;
a single vein multiplies to a spate
of interlacings, it's a waterfall

tricking from an elm's summit to its bole,
then staging flight-lines across a wood floor,
it underpins nettles, and mirrors light
in twinkling sprays at every catch of wind.

Dark berried, honey blossomed, ivy reigns
by rule of numbers, here convolvulus
has frothed the entanglement of a hedge
with white trumpet flowers, and a bullfinch

shows violet reflections in its feathers.
You smell rain coming on in ivy leaves,
their coolness has the sheen of green satin,
or by the garden trellis pointing down

each lance-head's deckled by a silver line
or tongued with yellow. There a robin flicks
an orange spark into an elder tree,
its movements quick in the late summer air.

Leathery, crisp, each leaf is a cat's ear
enquiring of the raindrop, a raised sail
running with the wind, or sinuously
darting a lizard's tongue to catch a fly . . .

Sovereign to woods, fleurets on a column,
it threshes with the gust into a wave,
hissing variables of green silvered
in breaking with blue tints of a fast sky.

# Stepping Stones

Gun-metal grey, plotted across a stream,
gibbous, hump-backed, aligned by an eye-beam,

raised stones fashioned strategically were how
we crossed from a valley to a meadow,

the split between two farmlands emphasized
by the change over, an unrealised

passage from childhood to a territory,
unbounded, riddled by complexity,

one's feet feeling for guide-stones, ways to cross
the flooding torrent, but slipping on moss,

upended, pitched into the flow, the roar
of water smashing flotsam on the shore,

no crossing place, no foothold on the edge,
the foment streamlined into a white wedge,

a line of power humming from a switch.
For years I stood with my back to a ditch,

a cat pawing the shallows, unwilling
to risk the turmoil, the whirlpool's snow-ring,

looking for islands, a winkle-black chain
of stepping stones beaded by the fine stain

of flurried spray, and came in time to find
those landmarks mapped out areas of my mind,

stones embedded for reference, still secure,
pointing a direction for the future.

# Goldfinch

Reading a thistle plume
instructively, it's the shift of balance
intrigues, the ability to touch down
on a resilient upright,
or hang suspended, bill dipping for seeds
that float like luminous islands
inside the pappus. Then the extravagance
of colour engages, black, white and red,
the gold in the wing feathers traced
like an isthmus of sand between two tides,
the fidgety nervousness gustily
displaying a fanned brilliance.

On horseknot, groundsel and chickweed,
they'll congregate in autumn,
twenty or more excitedly
feeding on a fallow tract – thistle drift
moulting into the underfloor,
a flotilla of silver balloons . . .
Dexterous, undisturbed they are
colourful as red admirals,
a late one visiting the blackberries,
its silk wings open like a star.

# Glow Worm

Green phosphorence in this hedgeside,
but fewer now, their lanterns hooked
to abdomens, the air nervy,
crackling like black tissue paper,
the simmer preceding thunder
alive with electricity.

By sloe and hawthorn clustering,
lighting up, sporadic flickers,
sputtery or luminous,
taxiing on a leaf-strip,
four together in a ring.

Abroad at night and piloting,
the male finds the winking beacon
of the female on a grass-spear.
Their business is the snail's helix,
paralysing that fleshy ear.

Points in the lampblack
leafy lane, the thunder rolling in,
cleansing the dust film, as we search
the attic for a memento
lost years ago, an emerald tie-pin.

# Bats

Pipistrelles stirruped in the barn's
body-heat of baled cow-fodder,
a musty straw smell of shavings
curled from a plane, the slack udders

of a sick cow were vetted here
last summer, gold dung in the stall's
dried to a fossil of the straw.
Beam-hooked the bat's leathery ball's

all rump, a tawny mouse body,
cat's ears, a mastiff's head, the wings
folded over the fur for warmth.
In sleep their axis slightly swings.

When they came back with the ferret,
the gamesack bloody, their light sleep
was the first of hibernation.
A lamp brought them up from the deep

of the black caul in which they hung,
nose-leaves twitching, invertedly
suspended, their point of arrest
was a dark cone of gravity –

a torpid count-down to zero.
On warm days they'd erratically
resume a looped eccentric beat,
repeated round a roof or tree,

like something without memory,
testing a wing cover's struts,
trying for partial recall
in that scouting flight. We shut

them back in their nocturnal dark,
and sensed an awareness, their slow
drift of consciousness was a drop
falling into a well below.

# Fermentation

The pond's the colour of an old carp's skin,
a blue-green filamental algae spawns
so quickly that the dragonfly's hairpin –

a bronze totem-pole with an Inca mask
of ocelli looks like a hovercraft
above a slick of weed. A water cask

scummed over, it's the green of apple moss
on rush leaves, the brown rat's bony midden
is particled into a scaly dross

of fish-bones, feathers, fur, a sparrow's head.
Their highroads lead from the pond to a barn,
a scored run. Sunlight picks out every thread

in the silver-horned caddis fly, its black
and white curling antennae are a stag's –
antlers, head lowered, sweeping to attack,

its steel-blue wings scintillate in the light.
A day in late summer, each brilliant
that travels through the water is in flight,

the wood-mouse scavenges hazels, rose-hips,
and chisels an oval hole through each nut.
A sudden splash and it's a moorhen flips

wide of the shadow of a hawk. It dives.
We take the gold-down from the mellow light,
we'll need it when the first redwing arrives.

# Eagle Ray

Duck-billed, a fleshy snout, the head protrudes
        forward from a triangular
yellowish disc; the shape's almost a star,

the tail's a sjambok with an aerial,
        the flexible crook of a cane.
Bat-shaped, eyes set wide, there's no colour stain

that overlaps in its buff camouflage,
        it is sand breathing, and there's no
fluctuation of a white hem to show

how resolution wins its prey, the teeth
        are millstones pasting a crab-shell,
or it flicks free, cruising into the swell,

and swims by flying, a bird-fish that zooms
        into a mint of nervous fry,
and gravitates upwards to meet the sky.

Kiting the surface above plankton rafts,
        its pointed wings and missile-head
bring to the light patterns of the sea-bed,

the buffish, leopard colours of a shelf,
        home of the monkfish, the sand shark,
the crab's weedy tank moving through the dark.

A shape from Miro, a fruit bat's profile,
        these rarely show up in the trawl.
The stipple on them's close-knit as a shawl,

they are the earthed mantle of a sand-storm,
        rising on impulse, then gone flat,
eyes watching in the green depths like a cat.

# An Old Score

An ox-eyed twist in each nubby conker –
veteran antagonists, one partially
withstanding a hairline segmentary flaw,
I still remember the finality

with which mine cracked, after its gnarled black shell
had been championed through three winters, the split
was like a glass exploding under heat,
a detonation that your perfect hit

followed through, the backlash grazing your thumb . . .
The prickly pods are down again, I pass
the stone farmhouse that you inherited
from generations on the land, the grass

is burnished with a fall of chestnut leaves.
You're working somewhere on a drainage ditch
through a beech copse, clearing out wedged black leaves
that block the flow, boarding out where a hitch

could have a rain-flooded stream overflow.
Ten years? I cuff a chestnut to a shine,
highlighting silver in that squirrel-red,
and darker hues of mahogany, wine,

the raindrop berried in a thrush's eye,
and feel again the urge to make things crack,
to level with you, sharpening my aim,
feet squarely spaced, wrist flexing to attack.

# The Way It Is

Razor-stroppy, lime-green, a nettle patch
with dusty catkin florets, brutishly
lays claim to a farm garden choked by weeds,
crab-apples reddening on a twisted tree,

the lane a raffish head-height of brambles,
old elms brought down for logging, a thin fire
threading out of the hollow of a wood,
cattle stalling before a ticking wire

that thrums with a low voltage. On the hill,
I watch a kestrel stagger in the wind,
stall, pan dead, then accelerate, its eyes
are the red photo-lenses of a mind

that scans the pulse-spot in a lizard's skin,
a radar-bleep a hundred feet below.
A landscape of survival; the old Ford
rusting in the yard's cranked up to a slow

downhill start, a black smoke of churlish oil . . .
I walk these lanes, things that endure define
not permanence but an obduracy
to live outside the age and not refine

an old tradition with machinery.
What lives on has its roots in history,
a throw-back, not a way forward, barn shops,
anaemic crops, milk for a small dairy.

It is the tetchy nettles symbolize
a holding on, roots cut down they come back
with a formidable tenacity,
crisp, arrow-headed, ready to attack.

# Swallows

For five successive days they've opened out
into the drilling rain, twitchy zigzags
of bat-loops, aerial curvatures that trace
a frenetic flight-line on space,
the crack of their wings snapping like blue flags
cuffed by a gust, streamlined, putting to rout
the sluggish insect traffic, a slow bee
stumbling on a cold-level energy.

I thought they'd gone, the fields stubbled red-gold,
a wet September, but their eager cries
were chasing, harrying from tree to ground,
in search of what they hadn't found,
the overreach that has them desert ties,
a black arc beating sunwards from the cold,
delayed here, frisking across a meadow
with such industry you can feel the flow

of current, surcharge in the beady eye.
I watched them from a flapping chestnut grove,
scything the air-currents, a huddled stain
of crows facing into the rain,
tireless, wing-feeding, now dipping above
the plankton-line, embroidering the sky
with spirals, helices, darting to catch
a brittle wasp that sputters like a match.

# Scabious

A blue that's lavender then blue again,
the tail end of the visible spectrum,
last of the colours that the artist's eye

learns to engage. Pincushion flower of seeds
granulated like gunpowder on lime –

caraway thousands sprinkled on a crust.
Who would have thought so delicate a ruff
would find completion on a ferny base,

the blue crimped to the fine pleating of lace?
I knew you wild, Devilsbit scabious

in grassland, jewel-eyed after summer rain.
Green inside blue, this garden sort I find

comes into focus like a thought that's held
for the duration of its opening out

into the shifting lenses of the mind.

# Hölderlin's Madness

At Tübingen the hammers ring all day,
and send the squirrel shinning for its drey,
its tree-top cache of green acorns.
Its lightning-sprint disturbs a shrieking jay,
and from the first floor a white face looks down
and watches blond shavings curl from a plane,
pine-resin, and observes the cow-eyed knot
Zimmer examines in the grain.
Table and chairs assemble, a cabinet;
he finds he sees things only to forget

their individuality, and bolts
his whitewashed room and listens to the jolts
a hammer imposes, a saw
irregularly grooved, spitting red dust.
He plays the piano; no variations
of scale compete. He is something hollow,
a vessel through which storms of madness blow.
He's disappeared to himself,
someone no longer separate, alone;
he concentrates his nerve-ends into stone,

and sees the autumnal Neckar turn gold.
The wasp is heavy, and the Spitzberg's cold
summit is blued with mist. He takes
the children out in a hand-cart and shakes
indigo plums from the branches. Are they there,
the tableau of faces quizzing the air?
'The voice in Homer predicted things right,
the meanest living Philistine
in Stuttgart, is more fortunate than I
the prince of shadows, living for the sky.'

Fever, the heat inside rocking his head,
the madness on him, he is weeks in bed.
Uncle Fritz, the children call,
perched like cats sunning on the garden wall,
but he's deaf to their importuning cries.
He sits, staring out at the clear blue skies
above the Alps; death is an absolute,
a graduation to the light.
It is the quiet in the wood when wind
has stripped the leaves. A new calm rules his mind.

# Finding Out

You knew it in the unexpectancy
of the word's arrival, the clarity
of metaphor telescoping to obtain
variants of how we see; the light came its own way
into the gold-drop of the stitchwort's eye,
the pansy's violet butterfly,
a coral branch of pink cherry blossoms,
and you were there to point it, recreate
the moment placed on universal trial,
and add to it a music.

A life of waiting in the shade for sun
to reaffirm the unpredictable
identity of things, getting inside
the sun-film on the fruit's gold rind,
the tree's crown of green surf,
whatever changed form whenever the mind
was guided to it by no preconceived
deliberation, and the image won
clearly as light trapped inside a crystal.

And if the way was secret there was one
who recognised, and gave the surety
that years on, out of life, he'd still retain
knowledge of your identity,
seeing you amongst crowds, the jostling train
of the underworld, walking a plank bridge
after the ferry, attracting your eye –
to get here it's necessary to die.

# Turning Point

Carp-flushed maple and chestnut leaf
under my feet on the hill's slide
to a meadow blued by a stream,
a horse painting itself in, a mirage –
chiaroscuro of the haze;
an arch of elders blackening,
elms decrepit with age.

A turning point here in the hill's divide,
what once was local, permanent,
the small farms and their tradition,
are uprooted in the landslide
of patchwork values, here a thrush
prises red berries from convolvulus
knotted into a thorny bush.

Pivotal here, I prolong the moment,
the savouring of things that cannot last;
the horse disappears up meadow,
a fieldfare rises from the grass.
A scratchy picture holds; my eye's the frame.
Autumn will flood this quiet valley
like red wine poured into a glass.

II

# Space Facilitator

He paints: a brush-tip not an aerosol
   adding depth to blue heptagons,
the cobalt deserts of deep space.
Since he came back to earth from a black hole,
   the time-warp's blocked his memory,
and when the flashes come he's still up there
in the orbital band for geostationary
   satellites, holding a fixed place
by swinging round the world's revolutions,
before the fissure opened, and his mind
   closed down at the enormity.
He monitors space debris, satellites
gone defunctive, bodies, equipment lost
   that no reclamation patrol
can locate – fuel-tanks, missile-casings, tools,
the metal wheel of potential fall-out
   conflagrating before it cools
on impact with the earth, the sea. He writes
reports rejected for their literary
   content, evidence of a century
consigned to archives. He is lonelier
than the first man, and awaits the return
   of someone liberated from a past
accessible to both. Time moves too fast,
and the last one to come back was charred to ash
   by some detonative fuel flash.
He dreams of those above who didn't burn,
   lost in indefinite orbit,
and how his contemporaries might get free
of the great rift, the cosmic trap and find
   re-entry to the stratosphere,
occur as a collective flock one night,
preserved, helmeted, touching down
   like migrant birds attracted to a light.

# Highrise and Low

The highrise faction dominate the low
from Cloudland, engaged in the industry
of aeronautical revolution –
their enemies are those below
who still lay claim to the earth, slow-motion
occupants of dust-fissures, a raised land,
and here and there an incongruous tree
affording leafy draughts of oxygen.
On skydecks they assemble red or gold
helicopters according to status,
and fly above the old world. Their children
have trouble with ground-balance, learn to fly,
and patrol fuel-rigs in the sky. They dream
of colonies in space, liquidation
of an alien species who still resist
their inveterate menace, and exist
as fugitives gone underground, who live
by instinct, the tenacity to survive.

The Lowland resistance are nomadic
autochthons of the cyclic seasons.
They stripe their faces with red earth and raid
the old munitions factories afraid
they'll lack a means of warfare. They are moles
learning to subsist in dark holes.
Occasionally a fleet of cars elude
the vigilant helicopter traffic,
and they shift territory for more food,
medical supplies, blankets, bottled blood.
Their limousines are camouflaged, they keep
their offspring in tunnels, rock caves, and sleep
all winter in a sort of primal trance.
Both fear the union of opposites –
a silver-suited pilot decanting
violet sperm into the anomalies
of an earthly body, and the hybrid
raising a new breed, a nuclear king
in the white winter with his contemptuous
impulse to eradicate everything.

# Terrorists

They dyed their hair platinum and drove red
sports models across Flatland, a new state
created for a species invented
by holographic insemination –
light-people whose infiltration
threatened film-archives, they were illusions
in 3D who'd acquired a permanence,
and coloured like exotic butterflies
in red and blue and violet
undermined governments. They were the spies
of photographic records, and pursued,
adopted additional dimensions
and grew invisible to the fixed eye.
Projected on to children born in space,
they became a universal menace –
an elusive race spreading to Washington,
and by degrees identified, a face,
the blue pulsation of a light pattern.

The terrorists were Warhol creations,
monosyllabic, casual to the point
of mindless dissociation.
They concealed guns inside tape-recorders,
and treated language as demonstrative
of a retarded species. Their orders
were radio-transmitted in a code
they deciphered with silicone. They drove
all night across Flatland startling a herd
of square-bodied cattle from square meadows,
their radar-scans picking up on a bird
kiting the night skies, but the hologram-
people had turned invisible, a blue,
a violet flicker shifting out of view
were hints of their dispersal. They turned round
and faced a flat horizon, a flat road,
abandoned their cars, set up a flat stone
to a flat god and prayed without a sound.

# Floyd's Package

All night my rigid concentration ached
above a screwdriver's hair's width spiral,
for Floyd had peppered the aluminium
package with heads that wouldn't budge. A red
disc on one side was confirmation he'd
been to and returned from the moon –
it was our prearranged symbol.
I worked until the livid red of dawn,

then fumed, and walked across a scrubbed outcrop,
the tufts were thistle-silver, and the bleached
bones of a rabbit stuck out from the sand.
My outpost seemed secure. I fired a shot
and no bird answered, and the silence broke
like a forced window. On the wind
flaring balls of static crackled
at intervals. But no sound answered sound

in this deserted security-zone,
stippled with nuclear dug-outs. I broke
into these for the food in storage there,
several contained dead physicists, frozen
in ice-vaults, awaiting a future code
to awaken their dormant cells
to a dead planet's overload . . .
I looked into the freeze; the preserved stare

of a bald man, thick-set, middle-fifties,
was a blue mannequin blocked in the ice,
a name transferred to a memory-bank
for the undead. A white calm snowed his face.
I went back up, my eyes fixed into space,
where I could see red meteors
swarming like locusts to attack
a star that blazed inside the stratosphere.

Then I returned to Floyd's package. By noon
I'd prised it open, and securely wrapped
in foil were minerals and microfilm,
and a cassette I would decode. The moon's
red light at midday diminished the sun,
and I sensed an unnerving calm
suffuse the earth. My blazing head
rocked to a black-out. I started to run,

and cracked open a beer-can to appease
my swollen tongue, I'd lost Floyd's commentary
and turned round. Fall-out was flash-cratering
the dunes, over which seethed the rising hiss
of wind. I sensed our and the planet's loss
and threw myself to gathering
papers pertaining to the moon,
and crashed into a dug-out, letting bang

the door upon the teeming galaxies.
Floyd must have cindered? In the dark I heard
the rhythm of someone's breathing, and threw
light switches, and encountered his blue eyes,
the physicist I'd observed beneath ice,
who stood there as though fallen from the skies,
pointing upwards with blunt fingers,
as though he knew it would. Then the moon blew.

# Bird Painter

Untenanted all winter, our sea-house
walked with the wind, and gulls left a painter's
careless dribble of white on the windows,
wheezily shifting perch like nutcrackers'
grating to grip a walnut. Spray would souse
the salt-warped timbers, but on clear days we'd
return, and idle a long time below,
watching the gulls nosedive us in their greed

to gorge our mélange of offal. We'd stand
the boat on a water of choppy slate,
glossy like starlings in our black oilskins
and look up at our house, and contemplate
its shift of gradient. The cove's gray sand
was marked like a snail-shell, and where they'd dropped
these black meteorites shaped like falcons,
someone had painted their eyes red and chipped

a skull by constant battering. We found
the iron bar wrapped in a red paint rag
discarded on the cliff path, and a Booths
gin bottle of turpentine in a bag
that reeked of camphor. Fires had scorched the ground,
concentric, mushroom-sized, forming a ring,
and in the centre, a disc packed with ash
emitted a strong pull, and kept twitching

at power-spots within our minds, a ray
that bent us to it, and brought us face down
into its magnetic circle, our eyes
locked tight with pain. When you wrenched free, a brown
burn marked each frontal lobe, and in the bay
a squall was kicking snow shoes in white slush,
but not a cloud bulwarked a lucid sky
of duck's-egg green. Then we heard it, the rush

of something gaining in velocity,
that seemed about to fall, but never did,
and maddened caterwauling gulls into
blind creatures striking the cliff face. We hid,
and trained binoculars upon the sea,
and saw nothing but our boat spinning round
like a second-hand on a pool of blue
in the grey swell. I listened to the sound

of breakers dragging shingle, and a light
showed in our attic, then went out. The drone
had gone off now and seemed to agitate
the North side, then asserting speed would home
in on our brain centres. Sometimes the flight
of birds was reversed, as though dragged back by
the centre of this field. Their wings would break:
bird after bird would drop out of the sky.

And even before you kicked the door to,
I smelt our intruder. Wet paint and straw
soiled by an animal nettled our bile.
Huge primitive bird shapes with boat-hook claws
were crudely painted in scarlet and blue,
and who had done this, chattered to himself,
and parrot-squealed, vamping an aerosol
over a window, and swollen bookshelf,

and ran to the landing hearing our slow
step on the stair. His face was partially
scalded on one side, and the withered droop
of a left arm hung like a fox-stole he
cradled from damage. I could see the glow
of the squall reddening, and something fell,
that made the house rock. He ran at a stoop
madly ringing stone birds down with a bell.

# The Rivals

The group contest a stated rivalry,
the men have formed a mushroom-ring around
a white garden table and elected
a president. A car burns on the road,
smoke billowing through forks of an oak-tree.
They listen for the fuel-tank to explode,
the last of their fleet of black limousines
to survive the rivals. And the women,
banded together, went off weeks ago,
their eyes and minds turned, bunched collectively
into a force impregnable to men,
they would have stoned an intruder, the pack
instating themselves in a sunken farm.
They trussed the farmer inside a pig-pen,
unlawful times, an eclipse of the sun,
its surface remaining partially black.

The rivals flew out here in chartered planes,
bankers divested of their tyranny
by the liquidation of currency,
all monetary values dead. They came
with bullion-stashes, shaved their heads
and turned into guerilla terrorists.
A rural population went up back,
burning the crops behind them, flame-prairies.
A war set in between the male factions,
their instincts bloodier, more primitive,
conditioned only by the will to live
and assert territorial claims. Both feared
the women's amazonian traits, the moon
inciting them to pillage, blood-rituals,
conception without men, and very soon,
the solar black-out came, bears slunk on down
out of the mountains; the group disappeared,
the rivals moving up to fish the streams,
the gold bears marching on an empty town.

# III

# Points of Connection

The hurried scutter of the subway stairs –
they angled you towards another face,
a dust-lit wind blowing about this place,
effluvia of a tunnelled vortex,
no camaraderie down here, only
avoidance, shielding of the eyes, dead air
of an electric underworld, despair
written in stringy features.

No respite in the crowds, the momentary
meeting with eyes that express sympathy,
then nothing, unreal faces on a screen,
the one, the many, blocked into a void,
freedom without intimacy . . .

For weeks I anticipated your eyes
coming at me from every street corner,
singular in the mad insurgent flux,
and went in search of you and found no-one,
my face upturned to the blue windy skies
of October, its holly-red sun,
trembling on the brink of a late summer,
glowering with storm for the clemency won.

# The Ten Thousand Chances

It was there in the amberjacks I saw
at the aquarium, or mouth to glass,
in the moray's voracious potential,
the recognition of a code once shared,
an eye, a gesture, something lost, and there
in the bird's silent watching from the grass;
the apprehensive moment demanding
I translate it genetically; revive
that depth-experience, a pharaoh's tomb
of fossil knowledge preserved from the air.

Hitting the water square activated
dormant cells in the spiral of my dive,
fish-squiggles, a morse-code of dot-sequins,
the first audible buzzing of the hive.
I had to let it go, I couldn't find
the frequency, and loss of oxygen . . .
with people it is similar, we search
for more immediate recognition,
angling for an eye or face,
and once rebuffed, return to inner space.

# Engaging Form

Horizons arch towards the curve of space,
the fluid continuity of sky,
stormed gulfs acceding to ultimate blue,
the ring of planets, meteors crackling
across the void – fire cooling in its fall,
the break-off fuming towards collision,
or search the nearness, a blasted white tree
is all that engages the eye
against endings which are not ends at all,
but rifts, doublings of the illusory . . .

The poem fixes all diversity,
controlling the panther's fierce energy,
the hurricane's explosive peony –
scarlet wind-petals shelled into rose-blue,
buffalo storming with a cloud of dust,
the shooting-star's tiger-blaze seen trailing
above a cobalt line of sea,
the word containing the immensity,
and demanding of itself a new form,
the poem's shape that controls how we see,
think of it in a horned animal skin,
looking out with eyes coloured by the sky,
perceiving whatever alerts its sense,
visible only in that clear moment
of drinking from a mountain pool, its ear
filled with the music of the galaxies,
the shy, tentative stooping of a deer
to drink from the reflection of its eye.

# Life Expectations

Green ogees of a hotel verandah
repeat themselves in S shapes in the mist –
vaporous swans above the black river,
each spiral ending in a bluish twist,

a tusk of lilac that's out of season.
A tug churns a grape-cluster in its wake,
the bubbles shooting; where the sun catches
it paints itself into a carmine lake.

The novelist looks out from his penthouse
at a grey spit of stratus; the red thread
that guides him through his labyrinthine plot
is knotted insecurely in his head . . .

Now windows light up; the baroque façade
of a hotel's screened by an office tower,
a liner's portholes gone up vertical,
the building hums with the accent of power,

its company flag's smog-bleached ensign droops,
and is somehow a part of narrative,
a questionable option for the page
on which nothing untested will survive

deletion by another century.
Reality lives somewhere in his mind,
a non-temporal state, and yet it's now,
of the moment, outside his slatted blind

the plot assumes its form. He blanks the day
and works by lamplight. The age drills his nerves.
A girl in a red dress crosses the page,
the car chasing her makes to hit, then swerves . . .

# Blue Lagoon

Your dresses spilled across a hotel bed
were like the hectic dispersal of flame
wind-smashed tulips leave – overblown goblets
cracked into volutes – yellow, violet, red,

rouge brushed on orange, a translucent pink . . .
Your monogrammed silver combs and hairbrush
were childhood things breath-printed by the maid
who shadow-waltzed with your clothes after drink

had fired her to filch perfume, blunt the nib
of a shaped lipstick, while you sunned below,
prostrate in the pressurized wall of heat,
blue love-bites lozenging a hip, a rib,

your halved bikini emphasising how
the briefest triangle of white remains
an isthmus between two reaches of tan.
90 in the shade. A dead tidal flow . . .

Your Japanese lover's black kimono
was old-world silk; withdrawn, unwesternized,
he wore white make-up and restrained your flight
into the wheel-spin of a casino.

Storminess broke you. He was gone before
the late summer calm hatched a dragon's egg,
and equinoctial winds folded surf
in white thunder sheets across the foreshore.

Wild-eyed from too many mid-afternoon
aperitifs, you stayed on, a last guest –
hair a blond ruckus, facing out to sea,
drinking your favourite cocktail, Blue Lagoon.

# Divergence

Our common pool of childhood, metaphor,
feudal pike underpinned that lake,
their menace working to a stranglehold –
snouty like alligators, green and gold

submarine predators, they held you down,
accustomed you to insularity,
our twelve parishes divided by law,
your snagged foot unable to free

itself of insidious weed,
the granite baliwick anchored
beneath white fingers of the sea.
Our heritage from which I'm freed

by reason of location, not of blood,
but in returning there's assurance too,
in finding the old laws unchanged,
the wren still buried on the village bier,

antagonistic boundary disputes
conducted in vicious patois –
the parish officer with his armband
about to goosestep and salute . . .

a cockerel running flame across the road.
Last year an old turkey oak's spread got shorn
in a farmer's vendetta, elms pulled up,
new sap bubbling in the old wood.

You're rooted in tradition, your children
carry branches of the same tree
grown rimy beyond burning, green
with parasitical lichen.

A sea divides us. In the lanes,
the dunnock has its clutch of eggs,
fledglings for the kestrel? – one will survive,
nurtured instinctively, and live.

# These Days

*for James Lasdun*

We're silver, disinherited from gold;
the trompe l'oeil of the girl's cosmetic brush,
delineates fritillaries for eyes –
a russet-tangerine linered with black,

the donna petrosa implacably
resisting metamorphosis, her cold
scrutiny relieved by the decorative;
the ersatz putto snaps a lighter flame

out of an alloy dragon's throat, her bold
visual dialectic lacks transference,
the sudden willowy fluidity
of a girl's waist transformed to a green tree,

or golden hair vanishing through tall grass,
a red veil flying, and in fragrant heat,
your pursuit ends in sleep, waking to find
the girl's the silk flame of a red poppy,

the sky electric with imminent storm . . .
So girls in preparation for marriage,
reviewed the quattrocento cassoni,
the panels depicting an eager god

ascending in a gold cone, liquid fire
impregnating, and awaited the night,
uncertain of the fabulous voyage,
a back arched over them, a turtle shell

glistening with oil by pinkish candlelight . . .
Another close-up, a girl with blue hair,
sheathed in a veil of translucent silver,
swims into view, and discards her beach-dress,

her body stripped beneath the pantheon
of pagan gods, sunning in the Greek heat,
while the beach wolves assemble, and by noon,
have forced her to a disordered retreat.

# Looking Down and Up at Trees

A leafy province, a tree-top skyline,
the jay's platform, the magpie's windy keep,
from a high point I've watched bladed silver
twinklingly glaze the oak and poplar leaf,
and looking down on trees, I'm made aware
how none are ever still in the blue air,
and motion creates an unstable shine,
you get the identity, but the flow
parts from the centre so there are two trees
in oscillation, one to left and right
in mutual discord unless the wind blow
from a quarter without fluctuation,
so trees exceed their aerial boundaries
and over-reach, their ramified sculptures
pointing upwards to where we cannot live,
tireless in their resilience, a green
whirlpool's revolutionary density.

Looking up, it's the branchline occupies,
skeletal or leafed, the sap designates
how a tree works with both right and left hands,
an ambidextrous seeding, and the wind's
the carrier of that distribution,
a rich fertility, dissolution
in hectic flames, yellow, vermilion,
that upward rush deferred by gravity
with the big pitching down of autumn leaves.
Trees are the prototypes of balance, dance,
agility tempered by stable roots.
The oak dwarfs how my arms reach for the skies,
or it's my eye investigates the light
that filters through, a circular shadow
skirting the ground, the bole laid flat,
both in the pause and the return to flight.

# Industrial Barons

A sky-deck of office windows,
a cliff-face of white all-night bulbs,
this man is working round the clock,
his scarlet telephone alive
with buzzings from the international hive,
he is Caligula, the man, not god,
the shark cruising the shoal to kill
whatever contenders survive,
the small fish cowering from the shock
of his ruthless, dragonized precision.

An empire built on bad money –
he is preparing facts to tyrannize
the board; no concessions to this gorgon
who petrifies, then chisels out of stone,
faces that answer to his own.
Up on the roof a helicopter waits
at his disposal, a gold dragonfly
with its acid-tinctured sunning pilot.
Accessions, take-overs, the despotic
barons rival each other with the remorseless
hunger of wolves who fight to death;
the silencer conceals the shot –
a red carnation opened on a shirt . . .

A car pulls away, behind shaded glass
the closed face of the emperor portrays
a savage self-scrutiny. His pacemaker
is overcharged, adrenalin
is shooting him too high, dogfish, king-rat,
drowsing beneath a silk-brimmed hat,
recalling from childhood, all flesh is grass.

# Roi Fainéant

Green sunlight and festooning lianas,
a Bal des Quat's Arts, new identities –
the bee-eater and flaming oriole,
the olive odalisque's silver bracelets

telescoping into trout rings, the heat
so tangible it seemed stored in his head
as pressure-fuel, and a street monkey's red
patches and churlish frown . . . by a slight shift

he was reliving it, Tunisia's
parrot skies, and that day on which fire-hawks
had filched brands from a grass-fire, blazing sticks,
and distributed them out of the air

into dry brush, and then picked off their prey
bolting for cover from the yellow flare . . .
Now back in Europe, a roi fainéant,
his Rolls leaving behind the blue Swiss sky,

his nerves resist the anonymity,
the blue places of exile, and tonight
the Paris Ritz en route for a château,
his deer-hounds punctual to reclaim his hand,

his coat of arms escutcheoned on his bed,
a mistress all pins for the dressmaker,
too occupied to know except the red
shoes are displeasing with the frou-frou dress.

No stimulus in the Rothschild he sips
beside a popping log-fire. He recites,
Je suis comme le roi d'un pays pluvieux,
a desert water-hole dies in his loins.

He reads; outside the brilliant moonshine
polishes each field silver. A dead power
sits in him, undispersed, crowned by money,
ivy choking the issue of his line.

# Kniphofia

A flame-thrower or fire-hydrant, the red
kniphofia inclines its head
from vertical to half dislodged, a pike
     fallen short of its aim, furry
with black boxing-gloves of the bee
     massing a deafening enquiry.

One way of seeing, and tangentially
I watch you bending on one knee,
the silk bunches in wrinkles just below
     the pressure point, while the black sheen
remains taut in the place between
     what's shown and vicariously seen.

Angles presented by a body's curve,
or petals that without reserve
become more hectic in dissolution,
     invite by curiosity
a way of seeing obliquely –
     red stamens, a seam arching free.

# Head

Spins a top on a circumcised
coral-cherry circumference,
blotchy as a toadstool, the tongue
erects that periscoping eye

the way a potter throws a pot.
A leeky grain, doric fluted,
the column rolls a strawberry
of sharp surprise upon its tip.

I learn under this moist pressure,
the snail's adhesion to the wet,
mushrooms satelliting the damp
humus of an oak-wood floor.

One has also to imagine
an oyster's passage down the throat,
a shiver of black silk coaxing
a conical raspberry nipple.

The oral spiral quickens now,
it is a cave I rise towards
with the shooting bolt of a fish
breaking water before thunder.

# Roses

Midnight. The claret multiplicity
of roses, burgeoning vermilion,
mother-of-pearl flames in ivory silk,
a gondola's lantern hooked to your wall,
its orange light pooled in the climbing sea –
a panther-sheened salver for star-clusters,
each wave speaking of the mythology
of islands, sea-kings in the undertow,
the dragon's head fronting a prow.

I hardly saw you in the perfumed dark,
snipping roses into a heaped basket,
fire-reds and yellows, infolded turbans
of brightest pink that later in our room
would flare out with flamenco skirts,
a ballet chorus, beaded with salt spray,
exploding round us as the dawn
prolonged its scarlet-cored fire-streak
above the blue insurgence of a bay.

# Drum

You picked white lilac in the purpling light,
your hair copying a laburnum's fall
of clustered ringlets, sparking chandeliers,
and cut generous sprays back from a wall
before the rain moved in, crystal flashes
creating a knee-high triple rainbow,
and brought their perfume back on your wet skin,
shook out a surf of flower heads in the hall,
stepped from your dress and stood there while the storm
beat on a drum and put the day to flight.

# Ad Astra

Moss on the lip of the stair,
the colour of Benedictine,
lichenous Chartreuse, spongy there,
benthos through a bathysphere,

green as a Sutherland leaf-light.
And you with a calotte of pearls,
coifed into your cobalt hair,
led the way to an arbour where

a tearose trained its apricot
pompoms round a claret rose,
and the hem of your twenties dress
showed a lace-edge of watercress . . .

Bergamot-scented monardas
purpled beside red hollyhocks,
and it was here that you'd recall
faces in the iced waterfall

of recollection, laced consommé,
a cabanna on the Lido,
the memoirs of a star-shot age,
my pen committed to the page,

your décolleté, champagne baths,
the maid ironing crêpe de chine,
first visits to the Côte d'Azur
in a coffin-bonneted car . . .

while I your amanuensis,
kept hoping for a rift, a truth,
a confession that would make
the social substrata quake.

Another day, a common blue
joins skippers on the buddleia.
'Paris, was it in '28?
a first lipstick for a first date . . . '

# Wind

*for Toby Eady*

Runs flat as a cat
on the other side of this dry-stone wall,
a pressure turning me round, cyclonic
tail-end of an Atlantic whiplash, flare
lifting a barn-roof in the air,
smashing through gaps, arriving under doors,
hurting the eyes with a silver glare,
running a trawler on to rocks,
timber and spar hammered by surf,
prow-down in a shark's gullet
of saw-tooth reefs trophied with wrecks.

A night and a day its threshing blade
has lifted thin top-soil, sparse nutrients,
busy in every corner, and no barricade
holds good against its madcap raid,
keeping uneasy horses stabled,
nervous, unstrung by the relentless shriek
of a spinning cone that could break a skull,
clean as the ribs of a lobster-pot,
lashed against boulders, force that can turn the gull,
upend the black bolt of the charging bull,
move house foundations like stuck clock-hands walked
by a finger round the dial.

Out in it, hunched low for cover,
the sky the flying of sheeted water
preparatory to jumping a rapid,
I go low as a stalking stoat,
feeling my way forward, holding to stone,
to roots deep as the earth, red-eyed, unnerved,
lit by the blaze inside my head,
wondering what I'll next discover,
a big oak down, a sheep's jaw-bone.

# Rooks

Rimed elms spored with heart-shaped prothallia
of ferns, a creaky wood with sponge-moss, liverwort,
accedes to an oak stack, tall masting beech
populated by rooks, a colony

that lives up high, and indomitably
maintains that locus near a sunken farm,
a yard's smoking fetor of cobbled dung,
stable flies drizzling, spotting down to leech

on cow-pats, a spiral of jerky ticks.
All spring the rooks were hoarsely clamorous
noisily building and repatching nests,
snapping twigs in strong bills, raiding the yard

for straw to pack into that misshapen
straggle of unkempt sticks and mud, a forked
repository for its green blotchy eggs.
The sow's piglets still suckled in their pen.

A garrulous industry, the young hatched,
rooks with their throat sacks pasting cockchafers
would force-feed fledglings, a raw gobbed spittle
of dissected insects, elytra, wings,

a crammed wriggling mass. Later they were gone,
they'd fly out over the country for seeds,
wire-worms, and one I found was gutted to the bone,
a wing-snapped victim of a carrion crow.

In winter they would roost, ragged festoons
would flag back at twilight into a red
December sun, their shape, a giant bird,
the stragglers at the tail, the fast ahead.

# Correspondence

The shaded areas grow less distinct;
the latitude afforded to conceal
becomes an extension of privacy,
what's magnified comes to eclipse the real ...

Our focus narrows; we illuminate
by directing a magnifying glass
on facets which are now familiar,
the singe-mark blackens the same tuft of grass.

Across two hemispheres our lives contract,
what we relate is dictated by time,
complexity of mood, things of the hour,
sweetness of the peach, acidulous lime ...

From East to West our unexpansive lives
dry into black ink strokes; do they relate
as signs to who we really are, or prove
the testing ground by which we separate

two fictions, one responsive, one concealed?
I knew you as the person you remain,
six years of correspondence close on this,
you telling of peonies, I of rain

cracking red rose petals into the grass.
We never met, our letters abnegate
the unconditional spontaneity
by which a picture grows more intimate

by the discovery of small details
establishing the whole. Six years ago
and stripped of fiction, leaves upon the tree
were less uniformly blanked out by snow.

What we miss is the angularity
of surprise, not the promise that we'll meet
this summer, next autumn, a pink evening ...
Nettles and grass have grown up round my feet.

# Elegy for Senta

*i.m. Senta Marnau*

You died at the advent of spring,
the storm inside your moonstone-ring
was cranesbill-blue and cloudy grey,
colours of an Atlantic bay
before it breaks white in the cove.
What can I bring to you but love
of things you loved, and poetry
our lifeline in this elegy –

the goldleaf on the laurel tree.
It's summer in my memory –
you living not on time, but trust,
propped up in the blue of August,
listening to poems, each would find
a new resonance in your mind,
a permanence you hoped would stay
wherever you went on that day

of separation. Your heirlooms
brought old Europe into the room,
Kokoschka's paintings, lead soldiers
from Franz Joseph's reign and the Czar's,
two horses arrested in flight,
caught up in the muted green light
of a desk lamp that cast relief
on Grimshaw's moon, a frosted leaf

of silver on the river's slow
admission of a wharf's shadow.
Small things, details, particulars,
define the constellatory stars
comprising who we are, finesse
and elegance was yours in dress,
silk costumes fragile as a moth's
dusted wings powdered on a cloth.

Flowers, life, what you arranged became
more beautiful and yet the same,
dignity and simplicity
create aesthetic harmony,
your self-effacing love eschewed
bodily pain, you were renewed
each time I returned, patient, brave,
thinking only of how to save

those you loved from the agony
you mastered with such surety,
self-disciplined to die as one
facing into the rising sun,
trusting the angel's hand to lead
you gently on a golden thread,
beyond drugged waters of the stream
where we are only what we dream.

Whatever I may write or pray
brings me back to your last birthday,
it was our farewell, your wineglass
trembled like a dewdrop on grass –
'Only champagne and poetry
confirm man's ingenuity' –
your affirmative flourish took
in both, a last cork, a new book.

And now the night, and the god's blue
cloak and caduceus leading you.
It's darker here, and yet our death
releases a firefly of breath
across the black gulfs one by one,
its dancing-point a coal-red sun.
I look for you, bright points of space
are stars recomposing your face.

# Summer Night

A template to the act of love,
the silken eddies of your dress
followed your body like the strings
accorded notes by a guitar.

You led the way through pergolas to where
the stone head of the horned god Pan
leered under elders – rimed autochthon,
denizen of dank ivy sprays, dark woods,
drummed from a tree-hide by a woodpecker.

A circle in the summer grass,
we picked our way around their barbecue,
you carrying your high-heel shoes,
your dress a cerise sea
that shivered when a curve defined
its territory, rhythmic peach,
st'll contained by an outer skin,
rubbed to a polish by the shine
of moonlight fingering your spine.

# A Second Try

After the first divorce, a second trial,
both reasoned against the irrevocable
separation, and met again
at a party. In the bedroom he'd seen
the toe of a black silk stocking
hung free of a drawer and he remembered
the allurement of his ex-wife's taunting,
and how his desire was reawakened
by finding her more beautiful for the pain

evident in her sapphire eyes,
her newly acquired reticence, and heard
of her painting, and saw as she stood up,
the familiar vertically aligned seam,
and forgave her for that, opportunely
inviting her back like a first conquest,
and felt her silk ankles knot round his back
like an exotic bow fastening a dress,
or ribboning an orchid.

# Hydrangeas Mostly

Pink, blue and mauve enamellings
of hydrangea petals, I try
three shades of blue, a manganese
against a cornflower-blue sky.

A lace-wing fly's transpicuous
wing tissue unfolds on a leaf,
a thread of mucilage connects
its ova to the underside,

a microscopic happening.
Two colours of veronica,
a purple and a lavender
engage me in a shrubby light.

A moth's approach would suit me here,
face up in a dab of gold dust.
Hydrangeas again, chalky blue,
I have to take their lives on trust,

or invent a biography –
unscented, too conspicuous,
12 round alps squatting on a bush
I measure perpendicularly.

# Suspension

Silence contained as light in a crystal,
a spider's vibration in a pelmet
might transmit a storm to the emerald
in its ring claw. She sits in a face-net

before the mirror, learning by half tones
and intimations the line of her face –
a heartshaped locket, pointillistic chin.
She stands up, paste jewellery swims into place.

Then posing, a mahlstick in her right hand,
the other pegged and resting on her hip,
she spins her body round, intensity
catches her pouting with a carp's full lips . . .

Now she's distracted, a red skate-shaped kite
wavers uncertainly, it's like a cat
climbing a tree by stages, lack of wind
will bring its dragon's mask down on the flat.

She stoops enquiringly to the mirror
and frosts an eyelid silver. He's asleep,
log-heavy, a shelled lobster's carapace,
his mind crab-spindles through the olive deep,

antennae confronting a turquoise fish
that takes him through a needle's eye to where
his ancestors are bat shapes in a cave.
She looks out, the suspension in the air

has the quiet of water in a well.
Starlings are down, each bullet-brained gloss head
is sequinned green and purple. A moth's drum
agitates her ruby's dark vat of red.

# Fish-Shed

The chunky wood block's nape – a perfect V
was nicked with crowsfeet from a hammer's head,
an improvised anvil on which we beat
torpedo-shaped lead weights from a mould-tray
on metal wedged into its crotch.
The two wire eyes were snapped tight by pincers,
the trace established, or springy catgut
fashioned for surface fish, a rainbow fleck
worked into a turquoise-aquamarine.

A childhood refuge – adults kept away,
a socketless outhouse rigged with a flex
to a hurricane lamp.
Woodlice and beetles termited the damp,
and spiders roofed the rafters with lace webs.
We huddled there by nights, the smoking cold
of our breath wreathing the lamp's gold,
and imagined catches, the August bay
alive with mullet come to stay,
mackerel lined in on streamers of feathers . . .

Our own lock, and broom to sweep clean,
an early independence, winter nights
of poetry in those imaginings,
then splashing back to the house through wet ruts,
to scorch cold fingers on spitting chestnuts.

# Marigolds

Cold-gold baroque leaf-filigree
of trees thinning, and you outside,
wide of my focus, waspishly
serving to kill that pink ball dead
in a white fizz of dust.

Red hair caught at the right temple
by a ribbon, your sound was mime
to me inside; I found myself
affording an apple a shine,
concerned with roundness and the flight
of speed projectiles that describe an arc.

The room was bright with marigolds –
a galaxy in a green bowl
of orange suns, my arrangement
was a still-life motion
around a centre, like the pivot
of your foot
supporting you for the game, set and match.

# Sharing Offices

Square bashing on a rackety
deadweight Olympia, a black
immovable desk-anchored hulk,
the ribbon snagged or going slack –

you'd execute a month's accounts
or two pages of a novel
that never earned itself a plot.
The carriage had a warning bell,

a manual gear-change. We could see
cars parked with the metallic sheen
of beetles on a colour plate;
the harbour-berths turn bottle-green.

Ensconced in a law firm's attic,
two bats flinching from the daylight,
we lived to outdistance the clock.
Over us we'd hear pigeons fight –

a truculent burst of colour,
or rain come tapping. A new boat
was a focal point to our drift.
Your Donegal tweed smelt of goat,

your shoes were mired from the lanes.
Remember our wallpaper's damp
repeating sage-green palmetto
in quincunxes, and how the lamp

created old gold on the desk?
You left at three and I at four,
my draft poems scattered in files.
We had our exit, a back door,

your fishing rods were in your car,
the day must have its completion,
the hook baited, the poem left
under a statute's deletion.

# Crash

Up high, somewhere, he'd heard the first rattle –
the loose stone preceding an avalanche.
15/3/82, eupeptic, flush,
his fiscal grip indomitably tight,

he'd wintered with a scarlet sun's
overtly cyclopean pronouncement
firing his room each day, a purity
of cold blue dazzling Alpine light.

So clear he saw inside himself
and startled at the whirlpool's spin
of flotsam, his pharaonic mits
were tarnished by the lick of gold.

Coraline lobsters on his plate –
things cracked, he sounded out a shell
to riffle its interior,
the black gut tinkered with by accountants.

Placing a ship in a bottle
was his life's intractable task –
money as a jet from a tap
connected to an elephantine cask.

He came back, jittery, self-questioning,
a loose stone would precipitate the crash,
the big stones turned in their sockets,
a rubble-slide before the flash . . .

# Transmission

Rusty bracken scrolls drop their spore cases –
a pheasant's lifting flare of brilliants
whirrs up, its panic too loud for the brake:
the silence regroups like a pond closing
over a pebble's entry, pike down there . . .

I stand on the road and a red mail-van
brings the outlying world to the village,
the stamps have migrated like butterflies,
colours from Italy, Sweden, Japan:
a jet trail diagrams the washed blue skies.

Things transmitted and received on this day
develop with the slow plottings of chess.
The near horizon is a sounding board
that brings space nearer, the crisp paperknife
leaves a line clean as the hem of a dress.

# Games

The sudden break, the issue into dance,
   a step leading out of the maze
of formulated habits, half in trance,

and half awareness, we had come to find
   the improvisational measure,
a tangential plane conducting the mind

to a code of release, the leisurely
   belly-roll seen in slow motion
of the nectar-intoxicated bee,

exacting from the flower involuntary
   participation in its game.
With us, performing was a means to free

the intuitive from settled habit;
   and in your photograph I see
how even as a child you didn't fit

the role cast for you, your taffeta dress
   moves contrary to your directives,
one ballet-shoe arched on a chair, the stress

allowing for alternatives, a gap
   through which you act another part,
and by two channels navigate a map,

individualizing what has been taught
   with assured spontaneity.
It's the movement that side-shifts, the ball caught

in reflex action, decides how we live.
   You shin a tree bark on this day
of autumn, bees grumbling inside their hive.

# Poppy Field

The hectic banner of a poppy field –
a pyre of scarlet silk to the skyline,
vermilions smouldering, Plantagenet blood
darkening the soil – this mint of red
blowing in staggered waves beneath the blue,
stops the breath, halts the foot before the flood
of hissing embers cratered with black seed,
opium dust smudged like powder from a shot,
the cordite blueing. I take in the view,
the stormy clash of magpies, quick swallows,
and light swivelling in a blade of gold.
I stand off, and imagine wading out
through petals scattering like butterflies,
red scallops brushed into a mad blizzard,
a foot scuffed updraft reaching for the skies.

# First Study of Peonies

Let's say it isn't really pink but blue,
a blue concealed inside a general red,
the subtle undertintings of a flame
invisible in sunlight, while the hue
of the crater's pronounced a deep crimson,
a cup-shaped flower making the demand
we acknowledge it as a mixed palette
of carmine, madder and cerise, and find
an equalization close to claret.
Today my peonies are blue, the light
directs my eye to the discovery,
and puts my conception of red to flight.
Half-blue, half-pink, I think the former's right
and compromise with what I do not see.

# Second View of Peonies

A fleshy seraglio, one invites,
a ruched meringue of dog-rose pink and white
crimped tight as a carnation. Overblown
they incline downwards, redder here than pink,
the best centralize the eye to rich strains,
a red excluding blue, a white that's pink,
each is a wind caught open parachute
tilted into a pink flowering cherry,
a beach umbrella at half tilt, a hat
I can't account for lodged in a low tree.
And is it fair your violet cummerbund
is unmatched here by bushy peonies,
their deepest red depends too much on pink
for any extravagant rivalry?

# Stampede

That night I woke to the stampede of hooves,
broken waters of a gorge, leathery
primal creatures, flanks steaming in a ruck,
protean, sooty shapes owned by the dark
that all night circled me,
so I was caught up in that exodus –
the armour-plated, tanked stegosaurus,
the mastodon's tusked elephantine bulk,
hide unresilient as bark –
the formative try-outs unloosed again
in the crashing of woods, a path cut through,
and then a dust storm whirring on the plain . . .

It was my anger going, the blood's tribes
involved for so long in warring factions,
dispersed in the tornadoing small hours,
the blind exulting of the thunderhead,
the massed dispersal, and strapped to a bier
the war-god's body porcupined with arrows,
prostrate on a red military cloak,
stretchered between flanks, awaiting burial,
commitment to the wine-skin of the dark.

And then by day, I rose and ventured out,
dazed by the thunder that had hurt
my head for hours, and found the woods quiet,
a single horse standing defined by light,
patient, head-bowed, awaiting my command
to stable it or spur it into flight.

# Border Pass

*For David Gascoyne on his 70th birthday*

Two swans tie-up beside a sickle-bridge,
their shadows anchored on a lacquered tray
reflecting sunlight flickering through leaves
of windy poplars. The air smells of hay.

The quiet of a village, and sunflowers
multiplying in fields to the skyline,
big ragdoll faces spiked with ochre hair;
wind has the furrow of the current shine

with silver chasing. Others have been here?
mop-haired, boot-blistered, wind-bronzed from the road,
the boy from Charleville lay back counting clouds,
his jacket speckled with moss like a toad,

Verlaine dragging behind, while poppies flared
into a silken flame. Is this Europe?
undefined villages, a dog barking,
a metronomic dinghy on a rope,

the local policeman asleep in he shade . . .
Go further inland, and the poet checks
his rear-view mirror for a trailing car,
he can't shift frontier and the border flecks

the nightsky with its military lights.
He stays on his own side, the cemetery
he parks in is a minimal index
to nations lost; moonlight in a yew tree

defines the hunting radius of an owl.
Something's always awake, its red eyes glow
in their nocturnal vigilance, its swift
rapacity scruffs the dazed shrew below.

A salmon dawn, the poet drives all day,
his mind big with poems, and by twilight
comes to a clearing. Three deer stand and watch,
berry-eyed, fluid in suspended flight.

# Overhead

Snowballed into a stacked dependable
debris, a quarried rock-tip hung over
a cottage with its sheer drop to
white water. Staying there at night I'd tense
against a shadow-murmur in the slide,
expecting a chain reaction
of dislodged stones to crash into the tide,
the big rollers cannonballing the roof,
the hill-farm lights come on at the alarm.

At dawn I'd hear the first fishing boats leave,
their inkwell pots and parlour pots
weighted down with concrete; their mackerel bait
silvering a bin of offal;
they'd lay their markers round the coast,
each the size of a red plastic football.

The tremor of an imminent landslide
pursued me. From another cliff I'd look
across at the pyramidal stack,
a blackback gull perched on the top,
and will the thing to happen.

Years later it's still there. The house has gone,
a bad feature erased from the landscape.
I listen inside now for the big crash.
The years accumulate; it's we who drop.

# Wisteria

Choreographed on a south wall,
luxuriant fragrant racemes
of double mauves, a lilac swash
of bubbles fluffed up by the wave,
pocked like the cells of honeycomb,
each a bivalvular seashell,
pasteled, sprung open on a hinge,
Caroline ringlets bushily
plaited or in tusks trailing free,
one way of emphasis.

                  Or lower down,
trained to make a low bush or tree,
the flowers invade by their smell,
a smoky mustiness of tea,
lapsang souchong, or bacon fried
crispily, distinct morning scents,
wood-smoke come from a clearing,
a bluish haze of autumn mist.

At night beneath a reading lamp
it glows like tropical coral,
while I inhale the bonfire scent
come in with the night moth, the damp.

# Helen

*after Paul Valery*

I am the blue come from Elysian shores
to hear the surf rush steps of the jetties,
and see the sunrise bristle with galleys,
risen from darkness on their golden oars.

My solitary hands recall the kings
whose salty beards I fingered for the spray.
I wept; they sang of victories far away,
the gulfs boiling behind their feathered wings.

I hear the martial blare's imperative
instate the rhythm of each oar's quick blade,
the song of rowers, tumult to survive . . .

and beaked on prows, the gods indifferently
employ archaic smiles the waves invade,
and hold out carved indulgent arms to me.

# Return

*after Rilke*

To know serenity the dove must fly
far from its dovecote, its trajectory
informs it, distance, fear, the racing sky
are only understood in the return.

The one that stayed at home, never tested
the boundaries of loss, remained secure,
only those who win back are ever free
to contemplate a newer, surer flight.

Being arches above the huge abyss,
and the ball we dared release into space,
fills our hands differently when it comes back,
heavier by the weight of where it's been.

IV

# Exile

Flint, granite, epidote, glass chips,
vitreous quartz flecked with mica,
I handle these and gratingly
evoke the backwash of a sea

turning its stones upon a lathe
of millenial erosion;
a shore uncovered glintingly,
its oystercatchers vervely shrill.

The haze lifts, I can see it now
drying like a water colour,
the wash leaving the house intact,
a stone-slabbed crow's-nest on its hill

above the hollow of a bay,
whitewashed, a look-out post, a shell
humming with the power of the tides,
the throb of a sea-bound trawler,

its engines drumming in the calm,
a red light on the marker-bell . . .
I live there intermittently,
gorse livid as an anvil's sparks,

the sea-change like a painter's dish
finding a sky for the weather,
amethyst, oystershell, charcoal,
the sea cobalt or cucumber . . .

Vacant on this blue winter's day,
the house is boarded-up, I try
to think of someone on that beach,
out walking, quickened by the spray,

who'll look up hearing a magpie
in the ilex, as I do now;
the clouds dropping before rain stands
a frosted window in the bay.

# At the Foot of the Rainbow

Part of it, lost already in the drive,
the winter's monotonous cobwebbing
of aspirations entertained, the lake
stood in the sky, so persistent the rain,
pressure twisting one like a tree,
an elm's wind-tortured, warped compliancy . . .

And now with a sky's bluebell colouring,
exuberant bird-song, swifts spiralling
in opposition to migrating geese,
new patterns dominate, the old rhythms
subside, exhaustion, the gourd's leather rind
replaced by catkins, green sap, flowering may,
spectacular sapphires lighting the bay
we drove towards; the clarity of air,
bright with renewal; the cycle's wheel-swing
stabilizing then smashed free by the wind.

And in the silver of the after-shower
on heathland, a hyacinth sky
articulated a perfect rainbow,
a banded spectrum, arch of humming birds,
a semi-circular blue-centred flower
escaping from this height, a dragonfly's
turquoise scintillae, the light copying
primrose, violet, pinks of cherry blossom,
and we, standing at the vaporous foot
of the unanchored bridge, lit by the glow,
watched as the colours lessened, a last mauve
fading like lilacs when the month is through,
and now inseparable from the blue.

# April

Proliferating variables of green,
dog's mercury and ivy sole the wood,
dock with its bird's-feather spine of crimson,
lime phalanxes of glowering nettle-heads,

it's sudden, stormy like a running sea,
shot through with sunlight, this reclamation
of a frost-warped, lead-hammered territory,
into a catkinned rain-washed emerald,

with cowled spathes of arum, mossed violets,
yellow star-groupings of bright celandine,
and in the hedge-hole a dunnock's blue clutch
throbs under insulating down. I move

by touching the informing pulse of things,
a transference of green vitality,
veins that are matched by tendrils, one shoulder
turns on the fired sap of a chestnut tree ...

Resurgent growth so many times proven,
but each year seen for the first time, a bee
hangs in slow-motion from nectared stamen,
a linnet branch-preens, and enquiringly

darts to a higher fork. The earth exhales,
its arrivals have come out of the dark,
deliberate, sure of their getting there,
occupants of a root-spot universe,

a speedwell's blue pin-dot on the planet,
proclaiming how individually blue
is the assertion of the unobserved.
Small growth unlidding eyes like meteors.

Outside the farm, a shock of daffodils
are bucketed for sale. My arms expand
with fluted suns, a blousy gold fire-storm,
rushing the lane with their dilated yolk.

# Farmdog

Hot nares to its greying snout,
was a snuffling shambles of awkward joints
in the sun, the belly gone bald
as a pig's, the fleas crackling in its coat,
splayed in the farmyard, shadow floating out
like wrack in slow eddies, but alert
to each footstep, ears pricked, territorial
aggression asserted at a bound,
the bark vociferating menace, and up
would trail one the length of the lane,
bring a cyclist down and agitate, teeth
bared, the snarl of it twisted
from the larynx with the congested shriek
of an engine coming to life after
the zero-freeze of inaction. Old scars,
cat-bites, nose-knouts, did nothing to deter
its officious policing of strangers,
a black moors-dog, bred with a doberman,
blooded this bull-necked mongrel's
baying truculence. Branch-clouts, a gun-shot,
its temerity survived the lot,
and was nursed back to a new ferocity,
its jaws set at one's ankles like a trap.
Muzzled for the postman, the tradesman,
survived without being put down, tenure
it got as right of the survivor,
to outlive its owner, see a third son dead,
and intrepidly claim new privileges,
a yellow-toothed assertion of its future.

# A Visit

The country bus idled at every stop,
incestuous gossip, news of a crop
curtailed by the indifferent summer heat.
We flagged on, branches flailing at the roof

and windows, logged to a slow motion crawl
by a tractor and its jolting trailer
indomitably holding to the crown.
It lurched off without signals, bull-snorting,

rattling its gruff claptrap into a lane.
At the penultimate stop, jostling cows
were filing out of a field to their sheds.
Engine off, arms folded, we watched them led

across the road, and frisked into a yard.
A manor house with its cascading red
swirl of overblown roses, a farmstead,
then cherry trees screening yours from the road,

an early 19th, pinkish-grey granite
farmhouse, its agapanthus and sun-dial,
its converted library a square barn,
rooms filled with the incomplete inventory

of your books, Persian carpets, rareties
of an orientalist, your thin beard
straggled into an ash-grey waterfall,
a line of curling smoke. A tortoise snaps

the black heart from a pansy while we sit
and feel the warm air colour on our skin.
Your land stretches on every side, courgettes
have ripened, lettuce, orange marrow flowers,

the scarlet bean-flowers spiral like sweetpeas.
Everything's here; I stay on until dark.
A squibbing mosquito whines round the room,
blood-hungry to inflict its red scorch-mark.

# Grebes

I intersected with in their seasonal
permutations – a reservoir's green flat,
a male bird with the arched back of a cat,

displaying its chestnut ruffs, puffed head-dress,
sharp profiled, red-eyed, gone without a trace
until it corkscrewed back to the surface,

then faced its partner, bill loaded with weed,
head shaking, presenting its courtship gift,
both gratified then resuming their drift

out to opposing dives. A day of mist,
I heard the panic of the fledglings, sharp
falsettos – the mist was strings of a harp

vibrating in the gold light burning through.
Cygnet-style, one fledgling rode on the back
of a parent bird, the other held tack

close by the adult's plumage. Cutting silk,
they moved out to an island; I would watch,
the unpredictable plot of their catch,

the male bird's ever widening radius.
Then winter, I would find them for a week
of storms sheltering in a tidal creek,

or round the coast, seen from a harbour wall,
low on the water, while a lowering grey
rampart of snow clouds packed above the bay.

# Pig Farm

We got the smell downwind. Oaks clashed like stags
in combat under an oppressive sky.
The reek got in through windows as we drove
from Tolleshunt Darcy across country,

the Essex sky a roof of flooding cloud.
We found the farm with its ramshackle sty
and mud field off the road. Late January,
the fattened porkers had gone to market,

throats cut, their obese bulk hung up in sides
on butcher's hooks, broad ribs slatted like planks
in a fishing dinghy. Mulch underfoot,
pigs nuzzled in the slush, teeth rooting out

whatever shaped their bite, their oven-sized
stomachs wall-lined with refuse, potatoes,
a cavernous hangar of bin-leavings.
You tell a pig's age by its weight, they add

a pound a day and never lose it.
A mixed company, large black sows, Gloucesters,
trundling, big-eared, all snout, unscrubbed, a sow
had littered in a straw nest in the sty,

the boar would show teeth to an intruder,
his trotters caked with swill, the clean farrow
ducked under her white belly, nagging teats.
Crows had come down to scavenge a furrow,

and picked at cabbage leaves the wind had blown
a field away. These sluggish, overfed
descendants of the boar were grouting here,
grown tame like England's forests. When they bled

the market pig its squeals were like two knives
drawn across each other, sharp blade on blade.
We got back through a welter of churned mud,
the sky above us puddling blue, then clear.

# Changes

You're under glass. Inconsistent seasons
have made this an expediency, the farm's
a hothouse aquarium of tomatoes,
sweetpeas, carnations, crops that caused alarm

exposed to the chameleonic skies
of an island climate. Broad of beam now,
the years have weathered your youthful figure;
you're patient in the yard with a lame cow,

your big hands bony, knobbled like a branch.
We've lost our thread now that I'm much away,
what can a poet do in the stack-yard,
boxing seed-potatoes or baling hay

our youth survives, the present is a gap?
Returning imposes a new exile,
rootless feet drifting through the countryside,
electric fencing has replaced your stile . . .

Homecoming means an appraisal of years,
most marry in a small community,
and if they questioned what a line can do,
the only answer is it sets one free . . .

The faces swim, they nose past me like fish
browsing the glass, tentative, uncertain,
in this game of who identifies who.
I'm thankful for the dicing autumn rain,

abrupt showers that leave the lanes open,
three hours' hard walking with no one around,
the sky silvering from a bean-grey sea,
my mind hunting a thread I haven't found

by the time I take the herring-skin sheened
hill-slope to your farm. You're loading a truck,
and make a valedictory gesture,
part dismissal and part waving good luck.

# Reprisals

A line of poplars lay out verticals –
their own shadow-siesta in the grass,
a plank-bridge shifting gradient with the sun,
across a meadow furry with catkins.

These same fields I have pointed with my feet,
their shaggy boundary hedges have become
the backdrop to the variant of years,
things soured, things won, a broken or clear glass . . .

Disillusioned, tight-knotted, I would storm
high-hedged lanes, finding comfort in the clear
spaces opened up by the fugitive,
the barb's slight shift in its red punctured hole.

Or by way of celebration, swathing
the hay's bleach of sunlight, finding its scent
in those indented eddies, while thistles
parachuted into blown silver spray . . .

One tried one's mood against the season;
each had its compensations, rainy woods,
autumnal chestnuts flaming canary,
the silence shattered by a shrieking jay.

Landscape as a mirror, but more than that,
a growth contemporaneous with one's own,
an exchange of trust, roots feeling the way,
the distribution of what's overblown

into an equalization. I turn
on the season's heels, smoky-blue to gold,
half in expectation, and half in fear,
light the heaped bonfire and watch the leaves burn.

# Neighbour

The nearest farm disappears under rain.
I keep inside listening to snow ruckle
into the welter of a thaw – blue ice
losing its jewel fires, avalanching slush
tracking downhill to puddle in the lane.

It is a time of casualties, the dead
mole who couldn't burrow back underground,
the wren, the sparrow and the robin dropped
from ice-encrusted twigs without a sound.
Fox tracks in pursuit of a hare's footprints,
end somewhere in red snow, buried carnage.

For weeks that whiteness blinded with its glare,
and erased familiar contours, divides,
and once out in the centre of a field
I'd lost bearings, and felt the earth spin round;
the brightness packed a land-mine in my head.
I knelt until that weird spin cancelled out,
and walked back, vodka-blind, holding to things
I knew from memory were there.

Today I resist the trudge over fields
to an old farmer reading the weather,
his seventy years light on his shoulders.
Survival's everything; he's never lost
out on a season. I can smell the change,
tonight the earth will harden under frost.

# Shrews

Hunger's a treadmill, it works round the clock,
pacing the shrew's industrious snout-down
foraging for maggots, its bird-like voice
twittering in leaf-litter. The least shock
jabs the blaze of a death-wire in its brain . . .
Thunder cracking an oak wood decimates
a colony under the lash of rain.

Light as the wren's flit, they boulder-roll snails,
a shrew's forepaws on the shell like a drum,
the snout hollowing out the grey cauldron,
or threading maggot noodles from the gut
of a hedgehog's spiked pod scutched in a rut.

In spring they fight and bloodily litter,
a warfare, undercover, unobserved,
the gene-pool working for ascendancy;
a triumphant shrew with a blood-stained bib
and torn ear crossing the hooves of cattle,
bringing ruin to the herd, won't be caught,
a gingerish omen in the yard.

Look for a shrew inside an owl's pellets,
the skull, vertebrae assembled, each bone
retrieved, tweezered into anatomy,
the processed skeleton survives intact.

Shrews in the hedgerow, my flashlight shows one,
about its business, sinuous in grass,
its weak eyes unobservant of the sun
I watched it by, finding a scent, then gone.

# Local

A turnip field steams under summer rain,
they alternate with marigolds for fodder
to barrel-fatten herds in December.
Blackberries ripen in the puddled lane.

They weigh beef tomatoes on dusty scales
in the barn-shop littered with old plough-shoes,
a rusting ploughshare, cranked machinery.
Good crop or bad the season always fails.

Nettles are waist-high round the granite well,
the lichened date reads 1934,
a livid red creeper arrows the walls
of a farmhouse; a collie wakes its bell

into a frantic tinkle. By the ditch
I find a celery fly in a web,
its green eyes and black and white speckled wings
have rubbed the gossamer silk to a pitch

no cellist could reach. I skirt across
a cow meadow; the manor walls are pink
with tumbler-sized, cascading, blown roses,
the square-stacked granite house converts its loss

of line into a feudal sanctuary,
its generations of land-income, rent.
Today it lives on dead money, its rooks
heckle from the crown of a spread oak tree.

I keep to fields, the redstart on the gate
is gone before the eye can register
the brilliant solar-orange of its breast;
the wild cherry is a purple agate . . .

Back to a hedge, too skittle-kneed to stand,
a Breton farmhand looks up as I pass,
kicks out, but crumples as he tries to rise,
saluting with a bottle in his hand.

# Separation

A dense green corridor of trees, no light
filtering through that packed opacity,
a tree-top canopy, and in the dark,
man still becoming, primal, physical,
undifferentiated from the tree
that gave him upright posture, lifted sight
to a superior faculty than smell,
and with its spreading branches taught him arms,
an imitative balance, later dance.
Above him, squirrels, sloths, tree-porcupines,
the raucity of birds, tree ant-eaters,
a world conducted in the forest roofs,
colours that startled, a dead bird he found
and dissected, and tried to learn the sound
of others, heard not seen above his head.
Slow beginnings towards that consciousness
of identity realised as separate,
the moment of awakening, the face
reflected in the pool not as a blur –
a challenging water inhabitant,
but as an image which was only there
as part of a shadow and disappeared
with the removal of that head. Man saw
his double as distinctly his, then tried
a stick, a stone's reflection, all different,
and knew himself as an identity
apart from matter, and began to name
things by articulating sound, and feared
the notion of his individuality,
knelt to the rough girth and worshipped the tree.

# Crows in a Misty Field

Vociferous, came down barking outrage,
a querulous fidgety assertion
of field rights – a heckled raucous mewling
that had drifts flap up in staggered wingbeats,
a ragged shuttlecock-feathered heavy
lift in their sooty numbers to an oak.
Others stayed down in the blown pink chiffon,
skeins of autumnal mist unstrung by wind,
then reunited, bushes of blue smoke.
I stood still waiting for them to regroup,
a coven's exchange of imprecations,
a tetchy silence, contested side-shifts,
before their pot-bellied resolution
had them stake out a territorial claim,
reminding of their primeval tenure,
their mortmain of carrion since the beginning –
a crow facing the first planetary light,
a black silhouette against the orange.
One wheeled up in an arc and was pursued,
undercut by another in the timed
contiguous chase of two butterflies,
and planed down, marking out the dribble-eyed,
nose-reddened hare dead on that scuffed fallow,
stiff with it, toxic chemicals, and stood
in a near circle, a burial party
in black mourning, cautious inquisitors,
waiting to tear out eyeball and sinew,
spade in like trenchermen. I left them there,
vigilant surgeons on a deserted field,
a blood-orange sun sitting in blue mist,
ebullient, irreproveable shapes,
sure of their find and unwilling to scare.

# Laying it Straight

The man is spading black nuggets of earth,
hefting a trench, I watch his overthrow
pitter to knobby clods that starlings truss
for the emergent worm. He leans his girth,

deceptively towards a point of rest,
and flexes to anticipate the strain,
a sort of volley from the spinal base,
soil-bullion loose-packed into a wave's crest,

a height that measures his labour. He stops
once to stare off into the clear blue sky,
an emptiness, a point of consciousness
outside his concentration, and he drops

his stance to watch the spiral of a lark
ascend on the pure energy of song.
It is a moment's lifting from his waist,
a reach into the blue, and where a dark

cloud crosses, shadows puddle on his shirt.
Now he renews the rhythm he's imposed,
head lower, feet wide, levelling the depth,
using a flat spade to pummel the dirt

into the gloss of a mole's sheen, and stands
back, evaluating the drainage flow,
the directional trickery of flood,
the wet soil blotches drying on his hands.

Root-wiriness impedes his slant, he cuts
these with sharp incisions, and twice tilts back,
cradling a cider bottle to his lips.
He stands boots wedged into a tractor's ruts,

contemplating work that's still incomplete,
while cows stand looking from a shaggy hedge,
with a wedged-head, wide-eyed indifference
at how the starlings run around his feet.

# Upstream

My way was counter to the gradient,
living uphill I walked against the stream,
the current's downpour looping at a rush,
addered with leaves, a contortionist's spine,

flicking out tendrils, a liquid ivy.
The hum of water lived in my body,
it formed a tension-field, a plotting out
of unresolved conflicts, a gravity

dictating an inner rhythm. I tensed
at the opposition, the counterflow,
the warped tree-twist the braked-run adopted,
an elm shaped by the shore-blast, rakingly

racked to a stag's interlocking antlers,
torsion and lathe-swirl in the twigged eddies,
the overlapping discs of green and blue
pooled to a topaz beneath alder shade.

The trek through seasons to a small hill farm,
the way not vertical but sinuous,
rose-branched, twitchy and thorned, the words I found
carried the stream's contours, its heft of ground

left broken, ridgy, reclaimed by nettles.
Later I learnt to follow the stream down,
go with the white race in autumn, and place
restraint on the torrent of metaphor

frisking the surface, leaves from the wood floor
lifting like a migration of red moths,
language harder to anchor in the swift
gravitation of a stream to the sea.

I came to find the mediating calm
between irreconcilables, the sheath
of clear beneath the current's lip, the pane
the trout browsed, nicking flies before the rain.

# Uprooting

Something is giving out, old jetty spars,
dislodged, unstanchioned by the winter sea,
a mussel-blue, sky-lowering, wall-eyed gale
that smashed the rusty bathing-rail,
and sucked the slatted timbers out pell-mell
into the turbulence of swell.
At dawn, the wind on shore, I heard things crack,
blue pines flying – an oak dragged by its roots
of bedded centuries out of the earth,
a shed roof blasted off across the heath,
pollards to left and right over the track.

I thought at first a wreck was being turned,
a vessel refloated from its reef-snag,
bullied by the groundswell and finally
blown apart in a green depth-flash.
Reverberations of the storm found me
spun by a compass-needle, jarringly,
no rest on that indiced moon-face,
the arrow's relentless circular race . . .

At first light I ducked low into the wind,
my feet dicing pebbles and walked beside
the stunning detonations of the surf,
each wave a wall erected by the tide,
but shot with light, an opaque greenish-grey.
The height of surf shut out the horizon.
I stayed on hearing thunder slam the bay,
head dazzled by the wind's resolution,
but glad, in spite of that, for the new day.

# Bus Station

The onion-domed cupola prinks
its insularity above
a multinational casino,
star-tiaras flighting the bay,

red bunting of a carnival.
Beneath that height, a bus station
cowers in a hollow; everywhere's
accessible, parochial,

magnified to a continent;
the four points are so far away
each parish has its own patois,
the old traditions living on

like convolvulus in ivy.
An island's surf-hemmed radius,
finds its centre here, a needle
at rest on a jerky compass . . .

A green bus khakied by road dust
arrives to take its stringy queue,
the driver waves a knotted fist
at tourist-car violations,

a flotilla of aliens,
sun-roofs down to catch the weather . . .
Above the pigeoned arena,
croupiers supervise the wheel,

tax-exiles chipping for big stakes,
partying at the marina,
bottle-corks popping to the stars . . .
Another bus pulls out and rounds

cerulean fingers of the coast.
Faces wave; a country policeman
books a foreigner, his rear spin
grazing the dent of a milk-can . . .

# Elm Load

Puddling its reflection a chimney pot
has formed a watercolour on the road,
shadows are miniaturists tinting there.
A lorry crane keeps dipping for its load

of sawn-up elm trunks, a petrol chain-saw
has sharked through the hedgerow, its high-pitched whine
an outboard motor worked at full throttle.
The bark's rimed seaweed-green, the end discs shine –

circles of white in which the grain's rough-edged.
They've felled with few omissions in a lane
whose gradient winds leisurely to crossroads.
The sawdust's sherbert-yellow in the rain,

big flakes that dust the earth packed around roots,
gone dead on the quickening blast of sap
that shaped the warped branch-twistings into light.
Trees in their upward drive form a veined map,

each arterial highway leading to space,
a windy crown. At each field entrance wood
is stacked for loading. A dead rabbit lies
stiff in the act of running, a dark blood

has haemorrhaged in one eye and bibbed the fur.
A dog will drag it by the nape and lay
it out – a sodden mat upon the lawn.
Elms in their roped up stash are greenish-grey,

split down they'll feed the fires of a county,
the sap still sizzle. Here they are on view,
pig-heavy segments cracked like worn leather.
Laid out horizontally they're untrue

to their vertical stance. It is an end.
One must grow accustomed to how the light
falls without interruption, the sunset
a clearer scarlet prelude to the night.

# Out in It

We've come this far, our edginess dissolves
here at a field's centre, tall meadow grass
greening our skin with seed-flurries, a stream
with nettles painted on its sliding glass,
mauve willowherb. The way the light resolves
things, points to us. For weeks we didn't talk,
now the green tiger-beetle on its stalk
provides a common focus we can't pass
without admiring how a copper gleam

invests that blue, and how a ladybird
adopts your forearm as a resting place.
A whitethroat somewhere, now a meadow lark
engages, a skylark spirals for space.
Things seen for their diversity, or heard,
force us to revise our persistent claim
of finding in the other cause for blame.
Here the yielding of rye-grass, ferns efface
the hard shells we'd adopted, gnarled like bark,

tough, leathery, and unwilling to give.
Time holds off, and small tributaries show,
draining from tension-spots; the light defines
a gloss-sheen on the skin. We'd gone so low,
we'd become antagonists in a hive,
the barbed sting needling flesh, but now we share
a note of levity in the cool air,
learning from the source, the directional flow,
that where the light falls, what was hidden, shines.

# Ten Minutes

A push off from that jut-cragged cove,
a buffeted lobster-dorey
took us from that point round to the jetty's
paint-flaking fish-sheds, its bins of mackerel

excess stiffening for bait, their green-blue
marbling turned opaque. A different side? –
another expression of the journey
into a wider stretch of azure sea

I watched brighten beneath the suddy wake,
my schoolbooks beady with pinpoints of spray.
Ten minutes to a jetty's weedy steps,
so green they were like the lime-leaf in May –

an ungalled silk heart with its pimply seeds;
and then the climb up to the garnet light
morsing an asterisk all night
to inshore shipping in the bay.

A dimensional shift, we felt the change,
the displacement of a friendship,
seeing each other ten minutes removed
was like observing a stranger,

the shield withdrawn, the face showing
areas released from the fishnet of nerves,
the knotty fastenings, a blue weather-rift
in a uniform sky of grey.

Nothing on this side, a fishing village
with its huddle of shark-blue cottages,
a spike of gorse-flares on the hill,
fish-spined, uncoiling into flame.

And then the walk back, each bright stone
a piebald nugget tested by the hand,
pushing our steps between three-toed
scratchings of oystercatchers on the sand.

# Lost Continents

Rocks slewed by the sea, in the undertow
I watched them repositioned, shape-lifted,
an evolutionary tableau
proportioned by the aeons, durables
whittled by fractions – mullet in that flow,
old as the blue Mediterranean,
blunt-nosed, elusive, once served in gold leaf
to an Emperor, prostrate in purple silks.

An alternative world composed like ours
is sub-surface; universal bedrock,
meteoric continents of the deep,
abyssal depths, we only see the flowers
of surf marking the buried land-masses,
or watch migrant butterflies disappear,
drawn to an island that's no longer there,
lemmings running to meet a territory
that's swallowed by the gullet of the sea.

And of Atlantis and its drowned sea-kings,
the marble and bronze statues of its gods
roiled into fissures with gold plate, gold spoil,
sea-helmets snagged in the serpentine coil
of vermilion weeds, was it glimpsed one day
by a youth netting prawns in a gulley
who lifted out a turquoise-stoned trophy,
and from that imagined a continent
passed over by fishermen, and the gull's
plangent outcry in pursuit of that hull?

Particles glitter in their uplifting,
in storm or quiet the one motion's change,
a stone oroborous round a sand ring,
yellow as a sunflower's eye,
a black grain of Atlantis travelled there.
I stir the dazzle, compounded worlds shift
in a sparkle of nebulae.
The lost sea-kingdoms are in every wave,
the surf's sculpting throws up fossil and shell,
cuttlefish bones, the Atlantean drift;
the sea's a prismatic turquoise
set above a black universal grave
in which stars exit and drowned bodies lift.

# Bluebells

Bunched in this vase take on an oak-tree's shape,
a purple-blue rucked foliage that's still,
cascading from a violet centre-crown.
Each thin-stemmed saxophone keyed by the bee
is luminous azure-veined indigo,
and lilac where the small petals unfold,
wind-stormed, unruly in their clustering
with small bell-pulls of gold.
They incline downwards and autumnally.

I came back carrying a thunder-cloud
of bluebells from Plough Lane, a scented blue
arm-swathe of hyacinths, elusively
slipping free, a small animal
I'd carried out of a copse, protean
in its grouping, defying a centre,
water carried without a container
was its stem-rolling action in my hands.

No change indoors, an ikebanist could
have minimalised on this extravagance
of reproducing a mauve cumulus,
a swollen shock beaded from the quick shower
I ducked between in silvers of the wood.

# Daffodils

A sun-storm, fire-eyed, yolk-throated,
swathing a meadow, rain-washed primary
colours, rush-green, canary,
enacting their own solar creation,
a glare that's molten, a blade's glass shimmer
on which the wind seems to lie flat,
then flickery, restrained to an air-bud,
before its gold chase puts a field to flight,
all dart and flurry, trumpets raised,
coltishly frisky with the light,
a coranto brought to a wind-stopped halt.

The way out of the scrawny sheath-cover
the green bullet-nosed compression chamber,
into improbable push-up places,
is motivated by light, the core-glower
exploding split-seamed into the flower.

Invasive perfume of tazetta narcissi,
yellow, orange-cupped soleil d'or,
the blinding fragrance of twinkling jonquils,
everywhere a proclamation of trust
established by their arrival, the way
directed upwards – I wade through stemmed gold,
describing a swimmer's frantic motion
at the wind's undertow, and then stand still,
leaving the circle spin out on an arc,
to pool a yellow sunset in a bay.

# Spiderlings

A microscopic colony emerged
from a cocoon-hatch, light as prickly burrs,
gingerish, milling aeronauts that teem
over a dock-leaf, paying out silk line
to catch the breeze and lift off with the gust,
blown skywards with small insects, pollen, dust,
the thermal updraft of aerial plankton
seething at swallow-height, the swift's scythed arc.
No sooner composite than they're air-borne,
restless migrants who know instinctively
to stay means hunger, territorial war,
five hundred spiderlings on a leaf-star,
testy, contentious, balloon into the wind,
their weight suspended, flown capriciously
across country or carried out to sea,
and keep no constant altitude, but fly
into a rain-wall, driving shot of hail,
their squadrons picked off by the swallow's eye,
its high-speed wing volleys, but still the force
governing the instinct to go's stronger
than the prevailing danger; these have earthed,
after a wind-plotted inclement course,
have come down in a field, separate, alone,
and watch the earth slow from beneath a stone.

# Wasp's Nest

It is the queen's prerogative to live
concealed all winter, brittle, somnolent,
hooked to a curtain or pharaohed inside
a wall crevice, pregnant for the event
of sunlight, the instinctive industry
to construct from the blueprint of its nerves
a domed-nest, pot-hung from the cavity
in a warped lime, the hexagonal cells
hatching workers who build the tiered highrise
downwards into a globe, a boiling sack.
The queen's ensconced in the inner chamber,
a big-bodied despot with crescent eyes,
black facial markings having her appear
in close up, like someone behind dark shades.
The nest vibrates; squadrons of hunting wasps,
wings invisible in sunlight, attack
and immobilize the speck in their sights,
and by late summer comes the frenzied rout,
the fire-tipped crackle of squalls breaking out
in ciderish weather, the unrestrained
mob, drunk on fruit, all sugar-fuel and sting,
intoxicated for weeks as they die,
burnt-out in the still, cooling autumn air.
The empire's abandoned, a hollow ball
without survivors, wasps dead on the ground,
explosive inner pressure of the caul
creating this, the queen a sulphur flare,
emitting a bass-drone, the fuzzy sound
of a devitalized motor before
stiffening by the brown apple's grubby core.

# Cabbages

Under rain and the smack
of big drops crystallizing
to beadlets, blue drumheads
with elaborate coiffures
extend in glaucous rows,
a furrowed reek of wrack
and compost nitrates oozing
to a puddled welter.
Most are leathery, holed,
deckled with a curt lip-
edge raised in defiance.
They extend in a blue sea
of uniform spacing,
some of them amethysed,
dibbled in drill-lines
to this coarse-leaved spreading.
Most have cradled their fruit
in elephantine ears,
cocooned it in leaf-wrappings
to an infolding centre.
Not a bird down on them this day
of relentless, sheeting rain,
I the one dogged, fluted back
for this shower in the muddy lane.

# Leavetaking

I    Cuckoo-pint for a token
of autumn leavetaking,
I recall now the broken
field gate, the red hawthorn
crowning one's crawl to the other
side of a meadow, the pollard
oak with its ivy ring,
a field baled in ochre cubes.

II   Those afternoon solitudes,
exploratory, excursionary,
leading to nowhere, but familiar
in their bracketing
light with the particular,
swallows diving the stubble
even in downpours, red belly streaks,
fattening to migrate in weeks.

III  Found by the unfamiliar,
a farm cottage in a valley,
I watched through glass the bushy clouds
the pink and blue of hydrangeas
race across the windy sky,
the last stook besomed in the barn,
the light fanned to a hayrick-gold,
startled to hear the lapwing's cry
prognosticating coming cold.

# Grass Lines

Fret-lines of seeded verticals,
tuft-haired, whiskery, bob-tailed, split
into downy plaits or busbied,
we had their names by book, the scent
of sunlight laid down flat in there,
clover flowers, green hay going blond,
spikelets crackling in the blue air.

Timothy grass, fringed panicles
of vernal grass, crested dog's tail,
each individualized by name
on thistled fallow, cow meadow,
our own personal inventory
of a green reading, while we lay
burred over with spores, carriers
of migrant seeds that never fail.

# Transitional

Indoors, scarlet gladioli
have the storm swirl of poplars bent
by April reprisals of wind.
The page that I can't circumvent

demands completion of its score,
words tested by the voice arrive
as claimants from the underground,
each sucking its blood-drop to live,

now greener rites of spring release
the busy wasp finding its first
scented nectar in the snowdrop,
partial assuagement of its thirst . . .

I lose the day outside, the light
I've crystallized is two parts dark,
and insulates a world consigned
to reflecting the solar spark

I've trapped to seed the emergent,
and recreate what's seen and known
by a removal from their field.
Look how the last redwing has flown

before the first swallow arrives.
It's in the air, the poem's flight,
wings, beak and blood, anatomy
feathered and roosted by the night.

# Summer

A flush of orange-red poppies,
rarer, Venus's looking-glass,
its star-shaped flowers sun-trapping,
blue cornflowers lost in the grass . . .

High summer? The days fly like leaves,
the century stands on its head,
invader and invaded run
on the same scarlet twist of thread.

A dust-ball in the galaxy,
we break up like an autumn hive,
which of the old team digging in,
will weather the frost and survive?

Luxuriance of foliage,
leafy viridian, I walk
into the centre of a field;
a harvest mouse clings to a stalk,

its nose trembles like a raindrop,
the thistle fuels a hoverfly,
a sparrowhawk combs the wooded edge,
whatever moves, attracts its eye.

We too are monitored, a jet
comes down low, our slow exposure
is sensitised by passing cars,
a camera details the future,

records our movements in close-up,
creatures who can't escape the lens.
I make my way to a clearing,
a deer's operative seventh sense

sends it deeper into hiding.
In preparation for the rut,
they've thrashed the velvet from antlers,
easily as a tooth is cut.

# Moth-trapper

A moth-trapper's vapour-bulb shows tonight,
a blue illumination in the wood,
gaudy wings hit the baffles and subside
as a floral paisley in egg-cartons,
a fauna of tiger, red-underwing,
a cream-bordered green-pea, the dazzle-flight
of hawk-moths; brittle silks come from the hood
of leaf canopy to enquire how light
has formed a global planet in the dark,
a fixed hypnotic point for wings to tap,
dusting the cone with filigree; the man
observes them spot, concealed behind rough bark.

We watch him from our own side of the glass,
looking out on a night interpreted
through long familiarity with things.
A breeze picks out a slack chord in the grass,
and in imagining moth-flakes we find
their impulse has equivalents in the mind,
a lost centre we gravitate towards
but never reach. It's curiosity
holds us to life and feeds us to the flame.
We draw back from a smokiness of breath.
At dawn the man's hands will be powdered gold,
his eye selective in its scrutiny,
freeing the known, finding for one a name.

# Brooklime Farm

Where the mad daughter leans over the gate,
an apple bulge in one dilated cheek,
pushing her face out to a pig's snuffle,
the yard smelling of cabbage rot, the reek

of sties, cattle sheds being swept of dung . . .
And all day she maintains her vigilance,
an obese, thumbs-in-the-mouth wickering,
or to familiars a locked silence,

running to hide when the postman arrives,
or a potato truck snorts in the yard.
In the farm garden she's built a tree-hide
in which to spread her treasures, a glass shard,

a magpie's feather, a tea-set, flower-pot,
and has been kept back from the local school,
illiterate, bullied, a cynosure
of awkwardness, her mind starting to cool

into a psychosis: incontinent,
she's punished and not understood, her hair
pulled out in tufts by a drunken father,
enraged at her uncompromising stare,

her helmeting the gate, tongue out, eyes huge,
conferring with a voice inside her head,
a raconteur who never disagrees
with the unlooping of a floating thread . . .

Sixteen or seventeen in a child's dress,
I'd see her on my walk past the farm lane,
once she was outside, squat-down, garrulous,
nail-flicking pebbles through a lidded drain,

then seeing me, gone like a startled rat
into a hedge-clump with her secret friend,
the one who occupied her life, while I
walked down the farm-track with its double bend.

# The Grand Tour

A field of bluebells shot through with stitchwort,
and now the chestnut candles pink and white,
birches are fragrant with rose, and a trap
loops up an avenue, its steaming flight

brought to a canter as the lanterns pool.
The stable boys don't recognise Pushkin,
his negroid lips, olive face, staggered hair,
his finger browsing on the diamond pin

that checks his silk cravat. Tonight he'll read
in the crystal library; deliver lines
censored by Benckendorff's spies, pick a rose,
and hold it out to a girl whose eyes shine

with mauve-shot sapphire, close his book and leave,
his coat-tails flying. Dead under the Tsars,
their faces stare out of beige photographs –
their eyes are fixed like the permanent stars,

Baratynsky, Lermentov, Polonsky . . .
names travelling like birch leaves across a plain,
poets on tour from house to house, white-faced,
monocled, arriving out of the rain.

Rilke in a Prague bookshop, Baudelaire
fogged out in Brussels, Lorca evoking
Andalusia to a student-group,
their delivery lost outside the ring

of those who gathered, intent on the word.
A pre-recording age, we give their voice
the modulated speech-rhythms that fit
our way of reading, or concede the choice

to a contemporary at a microphone,
the trans-Atlantic poet, jet-lagged, tired,
baring his isolation to the crowd,
his voice off-key, metallic, underwired.

# Space

Space as a convex sweep, a sea-shell's curve,
mares' tails and arrow-splits of pampas grass
are brush strokes of cirrus, high altitude
wind patterns, sweepings of contour.
I watch these vaporous chalk streamers pass,
and swifts in an aerial ballet describe
shifts of spectacular velocity,
chasing across the azure, printing out
the wind's directives, bird and cloud copy
the same fast curvilinear tension.

Days of unrivalled blue, with amber-rose
lacquer-whorls, cadmium sunsets,
a furnaced surf, molten troughs stormed with black,
swallows still holding to a zigzag track,
before a shooting star's trajectory
streams through a sky turned violet,
the big planets observed in their orbits.

Or else a mackerel sky's mottled blue-green
becomes by morning, cumulus summits,
a bushy, smoke-screened density,
the weather changing, and the silvery
undersides of poplar leaves turned over,
the red pimpernel closed; a pre-rain still
in which spiderlings cease to drift down wind,
and then it's coming, a torrential shower
that has a rainbow arch free from the hill.

# Sand Lizard

Is pulsing in a sun-spot,
its metabolic rate picking up speed,
a livid emerald lightning, tail draped
like a peacock's; the sun has freed
it from its unfunctional zero,
its hibernative log of sleep,
the unblinking brown eyes are apple-pips,
beady glass determinants of what moves,
ants jeeping out of crevices,
a kestrel's tilted shadow
quivering by degrees across the grass,
a bee finding the lampshade
of a harebell's tinkling glass . . .

Pondering the impossible
moves outside of consciousness,
it's polarized into a blank
spatial vision, until its screen
is broken by a spider's run,
or a sun-catching fly,
mistaking the motionless
lizard for lichen or moss,
magnified by that pinpoint lens
into something seen in close-up,
huge, vibrating, planetary,
a meteorite from the sky,
eliminated by the eye's
target-scanner – the inaudible crash
of a fly taken in a flash.

# Water

The sea's a mirror for the sickle moon,
turquoise and lavender, premonitory
of the September equinox, storm clouds
blown like migrating herds across the sea,

a big cat on their trail – the thunder growl
bringing munificence of rain, the lash
of silver coruscating, a sea-smoke
of boiling water lit up by the flash

of fish-spined lightning; how we live depends
on the elements, our small lobster fleet
cowers in the harbour – green painted dories,
scows, dinghies; someone on unstable feet

is tying up; a seal's driven inshore.
This is the union of the sea and sky,
the sheeting of two waters, and the bay
blinks with a dilated greenish-grey eye,

the storm-roads furrowed, unnavigable.
We keep indoors; the house rocks with the squall,
a microcosmic shelter winds howl through,
the confrontation of what's wooden, small,

with universal energies – we grip
wall and table, feel the house disengage
and walk shorewards to the fomenting white
wind-cuffed delirium of the sea's rage.

# V

# Byzantine Sonnets

*for Alfred Marnau*

Bad blood, mad Emperors, Rome's kernel splits,
the purple despot howling for poison
would bite the nuggets from a statue's tits
to prolong his jewelled rampage on a stage
the mob encircles wolf-howling with rage
to drag the tyrant round the hippodrome,
headless beneath the hooves, the blood of Rome
leaving a red streamer, a slow motion
trail that congeals and with it an Empire.
What can it hope for now but Nero's fire
to lick its ulcers clean, Caligula's
sword smashing a drugged lion's crawl, the last
boy-god autocrat thrown without a cast
into the red grit of the arena?

Caesar High-Priest, the old wine and the new,
the scorpion pincering the testicles
of the Mithraic bull gives way to blue
and gold peacocks drinking out of a grail
over which putti and unicorns sail.
Light has come home; the open nenuphar
proclaim it; the gold of the aureole's
reflected in the city's domes, angels
and satyrs chase the punished copper bells.
Constantine is withdrawn; he meditates
on polo and a rain-pasteled rainbow
spanning the world, the skies, if it was so . . .
Wind gusts the courtyard fountain. It is late.

Contentious nerves design his mood. His toe
stubbed the shaved Emir's skull, his giant hand
has cupped so many tiny feet he knows
how to keep a slave girl awake all night,
her waist dancing with jewels, each facet's light
a glinting ruby or turquoise, the spark
of an emerald lighting up the dark,
their bodies breaking like storm surf on sand.
His head rests on the neck of Apollo –
a flighted statue touched by the moon's snow.
Lord of the Black Sea how they chant for you,
Stella Maris, your purple sailed dromond
nods with its plumes, the water a silked pond,
the gold oars silently dipping the blue.

A golden egg, Hagia Sophia, red deer
browse above blue waters; each icon mints
an inner purity of life so clear
the eye confuses gold with crystal, death
is nothing but a diamond formed by breath.
If you would live castration is the art
to win an Emperor's or Empress's heart,
castrates knew Cleopatra's curved imprint,
vasectomy makes them into athletes,
gold-dust sprinkling their armpits and their feet.
Wars, accessions, swashbuckling emperors
branded with molten icons died like beasts
consumed by poison juices at a feast,
their staring eyeballs bloated with terror.

The Emperor cannot sleep. Justinian
paces the corridor, his butcher's arm
is too bloody for the name of Christian.
Even Theodora's lithe expertise
at flipping on her stomach cannot ease
this man's contained fury, her last silk veil
lies fluttering from a painted toe-nail,
her sated snake's body has lost its charm,
this she-bitch, once a circus prostitute,
twists like ivy for the imperial loot,
and flicks each diamond with her tongue. His heel
has churned dismounted scarabs in the dust
as food for vultures. Now she tempts his lust
by wearing a blue jewel in her navel.

Pillage, ransacking, Justinian would set
nations at each other, then like a stoat
drag each into submission. How he frets
to think a Roman lives, he'd drink their blood
and have Belisarius stamp the mud
of five days riding in a Roman nose.
Cut-throats, secret spies, soldiers, only those
who have an inner light can keep afloat
above a dark tideline. He does not eat,
jealous a slave tickles his elf-queen's feet,
her laughter reaching an enmaddened pitch,
and storms her bedroom slashing here and there
only to find the room empty. His stare's
that of a man cut down, hurled in the ditch . . .

Look up, the star-shine of the artisan's
intricate as a spider's web, detail
so masterful, the vision is not man's . . .
Constantine stares but cannot see his hands,
then howls facing his inner dark, quicksands
that undulate; the white-hot poker-tip
put out his eyes as he bit through his lip,
and tilted against a retreating wall.
Insurrection and calm. Over it all
God keeps a watch on his imperial
city of gold. Embattled sisters rule,
Zoe hip-angling for a Grecian stud,
and Theodora counting out a flood
of gold coins like a child playing at school.

War and the cloister, eunuchs massage oil
into the hairshirted Nicephorus.
Spindle shanks, pepper-and-salt beard, long toil
has made him morose; he swings gouty feet.
One stare from this man promises defeat –
a rugged general turned Emperor
with a sultry enchantress draping furs
over her olive body's kittenish
enticements, he fumes in the great divide
between civility and churlish pride.
New campaigns, intrigues in his own palace,
he wanted God but found a sword instead . . .
John Zimisces killed him, held up his head
and publicly spat in the dead man's face.

They say the lion and his whelp will rout
the onager. The city is a glass
in which angels swim, men must turn about
and face heretics on every frontier,
hordes advance into a black wedge of spears.
Bohemond presses down his Norman thumb
until the Emperor's pulse-spots go numb,
there's not a green blade in the scarlet grass.
Irene Ducas, red, gold and blue they wait,
heralds and pages for a birth that's late –
Anna Comnena, they anticipate
your wearing the diadem, already
they lead you through jewelled halls of porphyry
across mosaics to the Golden Gate.

An Empire blown. The star of Christendom
singes like a gold moth, blood shrieking Turks
whip their horses into the red maelstrom
of fire and carnage, look, they smash a breach
and come on as though they would overreach
the city and lay claim to West and East,
swarming it like dogs dragging down a beast
gone lame. These rapine soldiers are beserk
for women, loot, what can't be burnt is cut
to tatters, heaped and booted in the rut
of steaming flesh, Hagia Sophia aflame,
only the women are preserved, icons
are balled to fragments by bars of iron.
You look for this city? It has no name.

VI

# Between Territories

A gnat-swarm fuzzes in the elder scent,
a tennis-racket shape of muzzy dots
composing an indecipherable score,
an aerial morse transcribed on clammy air.
This is the face-veil I adopt, and push
through midge-flak, through the thicket's door
to smudge, leaf-screening, the contained surf-roar
of wind in oak-crowns; there are underworks –
the badger's honey-toothed sleep,
tracks that I left myself, uncrossed, a spoor
of scent I laid out in the black-laked dark,
oddly my own, conspicuous,
the first man's, last man's to appear,
each an arrow-point veined with fear.

That was the going in, the coming out
hurts in the light-glare, sudden exposure;
the chemistry had reacquired earth-roots,
leaf camouflage, a grafting of the skin
to bark, assimilation with leaf shoots,
the sap's upward drive, its dissolution.
Leafy, centaurish, crow-eyed, grub-beaky,
I could have waited for the transformation,
delayed in the green light for fur-padded toes,
wet sniffing nostrils, newly attuned ears,
but chose to come back, startled in the brake,
posting myself upright against a tree,
leaving my blood clear among dark ivy,
smelling of wind, cold stone, bitter aloes.

# Rockpool

An enclave, a blue monocle,
this one's transpicuous oval
is pitted into quartzed granite.
An oceanic garden culled

from the Atlantic's grey eyeball,
its red dahlia anemone
radiates like a salmon sun
beside the starfish, blue mussel.

That sudden flash of tropical
brilliance is a corkwing wrasse,
a jewel-flare of turquoise and gold
igniting from skeins of black wrack.

The pool's a Star Ushak carpet,
petrified forests of maroon
coral weed fringe mauve caragheen,
shrimps cluster round a sea lettuce;

the topshell is a turbanned moon.
A sideways undercover shift
of moving weed is a shorecrab,
guerilla-helmeted, pincers –

a medieval armoury . . .
Paralysed by stinging cells shot
by the beadlet anemone,
an unsuspecting rock blenny

lies on its scarlet death-cushion.
The hermit crab nestles inside
an empty whelk shell, occupants
and things left captive by the tide

must learn to miniaturize, live
as intertidal fugitives.
I keep my shadow off this pool,
the sky's a cerulean transfer

capping it like a lily pad.
Light directs me to what I find
in this mosaic, a grey cloud
shuts me out like a drawn-up blind . . .

# Curiosities

Persistent, in a great hurry,
the cavefish rounds its territory,
lateral line senses, crimson veins
hatching its pink transparency,

it feels its way by opposing
pressure, and that's a form of sight,
seeing by contact with a wall,
tactility translated into light.

The spotted sea-hare's raspberry
smoke-screen's an imitative shape,
a simulacrum, as blue ink
facilitates the squid's escape,

cloudy ink whorls as tentacles.
So nature's ingenuity
has a woodpecker finch employ
a cactus spine and searchingly

probe dead bark for insect larvae.
Patiently the green heron baits
the pool with crusts of retrieved bread,
and projecting no shadow waits

for a browsing fish to enquire.
Earth totems of the termite's nest,
the fan-worm's red chieftain's head-dress,
the hoopoe's spectacular crest,

curiosities brought to light
from the universal mosaic.
Black kites spiral with burning sticks
into an aerial attack,

routing their prey; the bowerbird
builds a courtship stage to arrest
its partner by shells, bones, bright flowers
arranged in its exotic nest.

# Flowering Currant

Quite suddenly the lane's a wind-rushed red
of flower clusters, a hedgerow transformed
into a pungent lime-scented pink wash,
a logan berry opening with gold eyes
into a carmine spray; they brush my head
in scenting their enlivenment,
a cummerbund sashing the nettle-green
of moth-shaped leaves, and as an overhang,
white hawthorn frothed into a curd of swash.

What brings me back's our common survival,
the assurance that we're both here and now,
despite the years, the index of changes,
a world no longer accepted on trust,
two weeks of such flowering extravagance,
affirmative red blossom that I breathe
on our planet's tremulous crust;
glad of our coinciding, while I cut
sprays to familiarize fragrance
at nightfall when the violet's spur snaps shut.

# Flight

The eye can't hold their frenetic flight-course,
swallows loopy as bats in the twilight
are picking off aerial plankton, a ball

of crackling insects pasted in the craw,
elytra, sting-cartridges, brittle wings,
the live crackle of furry abdomens.

For her, it's another trajectory –
an arc choreographed internally,
she spins off inside, and the flight describes

a curve. It is as though her levity
involved the leaving of matter behind,
her dress performing without a body,

a sheath of silk dancing into the wind.
A woman alone on the beach, it's gulls
that stretch her to the reaches of her mind.

# The Gold Bug

*for James Lasdun*

The powder-trail of white dust that he sniffs
on transatlantic flights elucidates
the grey honeycomb of his brain,
a sea-sponge charged with electric flashes,

a pitted Atlantean crater
telescoping up to the blue above
cloud canyons, massive levellings of wind.
A gold bracelet, ring, monogrammed lighter,

an Inca sun-spot dazzles on his wrist,
he is cool silver changing into gold,
the abacus of Wall Street, the Exchange,
compute holistic schemas in his mind –

that ersatz red suite at the London Ritz,
he'd stood the air stewardess upside down,
a black Puerto Rican can-can dancer,
ten grand on Ruby Ballet bullet-blown

at the last fence . . . the blue ice wearing thin.
He has to find the gold vein in the dark
of sagging bank vaults, the apple's gold rind,
prospectors have left knives in the tree's bark . . .

The sunset burns to a ferocious red
ball in his window. He dreams of money,
copious as the autumn fall of leaves,
the metallurgist's film of gold on lead.

# On the Turn

A ton of bronze muscles compressed to this –
the hand-balance of your heirloom Atlas,
a Cretan statuette demanding light,
an eye's appraisal.

In a flat beret you hold the window,
the thrush is spotted like an ocelot,
the winter jasmine's managed yellow stars.

Where are they, faces in the photograph?

One stepping from a car
could be sprinkled out of a pepper-pot,
ash of a hecatomb. They disappeared
unnoticed as the tags in a rose garden.

You press upon the moment, it is now.
You've changed. The window's steamed off your past life.

# Layer Marney

Skylarks, a pipit, a grey murex-whorl
of cloud articulated in a swirl
above a barned field,
lean-tos, beam-rickety, a scalded pig
hung from an iron hook for a holly crown.

Space resisted by a hall and its church
with three stone effigies –
the Lords of Marney and their high estate,
kingly, one bloodied on the cloth of gold,
like the pig's gash, hot butchery.

Oaks royally leafing,
a pink cherry shaped like a parasol,
and stockstill, garnet-eyed, a sparrowhawk
telescoping.

We wait for the squall's driving whiplash,
the whole landscape swept into wet brushstrokes,
everything pointed with the blast
to a storm-tendril, an arrested curve
in which the emerald wind-flash
of fields take off out of a feudal close
where the Lords Marney were brought back to lie
arrowed with thorns, wounds petalled like a rose.

# Sinking In

Nettles – an angry glare-shock in the lane,
bottle-green, adderish, tetchy,
a clump that invited recollection,

pulled me up as a stopping-place, a mark
of reflection, before the bend ironed
into a road knobby with acorn cups,
so much thought sunk into their glower,
their twitchy florets.

So much shared without reciprocation,
what I recall is blue September smoke,
losses, the evocation of someone,
known, and familiar with this place,
who looked through the nettles and never saw
whatever lived between that group and me
and remains finally.

# Answer

Corymbs of laburnum
pead-concertinas,
snaking through lilac,
a ringleted waterfall.

Over and again,
listen for the tree's oracle,
out of the beech, the rattle
of a green woodpecker,
place where I holed a letter
in the lichened bole,
and waited three months for your answer
that never came with its pink ribbon
and jay's feather.

Cloud shadows work my page,
their smokiness reminds me
of you untoeing
the film of a silk stocking.

The bird note again,
premonitory of rain,
and somewhere your eyes
watching unseen,
hair full of poplar catkins
twitching into the green.

# Parkland

Tail-up, inquisitive, a squirrel bounds
across the path and sits before my feet,
hands cupped, a demonstrative entreaty
for food; too tame, too vulnerably exposed,
it runs beside me, then drops back
and disappears along a grassy track.

Orange azaleas bushed against thunder
are livid in the purple light. I see
the colour deepen in a chestnut tree,
a livid green turn to avocado,
while blue suffuses a red peony,
the dullness exposing the secondary
colours inherent in the first, a crow
climbs hoarsely to a plane tree top and shouts
at the advancing tide of indigo . . .

Everyone's decamping, the avenues
jostle with summer clothes, they're going home,
a girl in a white bikini slips through
the trees like a fish playing in the blue,
two children punt a red ball in the air,
snag it in a tree-top and leave it there . . .

I walk to a Japanese garden, shrubs
islanded on a lake, a bronze eagle
stoops to its own reflection, and red carp
rise to the fissures between wing pinions.
The rain blows in out of a copper sky,
great yellow flags bend to the water's sheen,
my squirrel reappears, bolts for cover,
a fur-tailed lightning shooting vertically
into a chestnut's vaulted blousy green.

# Ferns

On woody stems, resilient, green lace
in some is leathery, the fingers trace

fine-toothed serrations, the question-mark curl
at the tip of Hart's tongue, whose leaves unfurl

into elongated sail shapes, I see
lance-tipped coronets of polypody,

gold-spotted, rooted in dead bark, the wet
affording them their firm, defiant set

in January, the path packed with leaf dross,
only the emerald of ferns and moss

vestigial of green life, feathery
leaves of the hard shield fern on rock and tree

arching into a calligraphic spray,
the wood suddenly stormed by a loud jay's

oak-top dementia. Here by a loose wall,
glossy black spleenwort forms a waterfall

of fronds trained from a purple stalk. The hedge
is leafless, everything's defined by edge,

angular, cutting, like the fern's notched key,
the spiky crackle of the sheened holly.

# Pacts

With most, the secrecy's a double life,
a wolf-shadow, the invisible vein
lost in the choking multiplicity
of ivy, and renewed over again
by black water of its underground source,
an ice-chilled runnel untouched by the sun,
the bottomless unmirrored reservoir.

Singular or obsessive, what is done
won't disappear, and so is returned to,
the assignation that leads to blackmail,
the degradation of a man broken
by something stronger than himself, turned out
to founder on the surface of his skin.
Men try to take their secrets into death,
a black butterfly mounted on a pin.

With some the pact's between glass and bottle,
whisky measures with no constraining count,
the impulse terrible at night, alone.
Duplicities, the need to keep concealed
the unshareable, weighted with a stone.
Love, fraud, the signature upon a line,
irrevocable in its consequence,
the daily battle with the blind cave-fish,
consigning it to a dark location.

Those who get through must follow to the end,
breast the cold stream, or face up to a wall,
become themselves or it in the exchange
at death; the captive out is it despatched
or judged, animal running through the hall,
dislaired, identified, the knowledge clear
both of its resilience and its fall.

# Wren

Discernible the way one sees
a field-mouse flicker through ivy,
the hop and flutter of the wren's
untiringly assiduous,

beaking the earth-creviced spider,
the blue hypnotics of the fly's
zany iridescences.
The gun-sight of its hazel eyes,

the twinkle of a jewelled planet,
the stumped tail has the rufous fleck
of a kestrel or pheasant.
Bull-hearted in a bell-body,

its pugilistic vigilance
will see a starling from its nest.
A little troglodyte in snow,
it disappears into hollows,

scratchy, stabbing, rooting for seeds,
the temperature minus zero,
its body lit up by the speed
of its nattering heart pistons.

From ivy bush to bush I watch,
the incessant activity
of this diminutive hunter's
dive and dart rapacity.

Its territory's a low flying
reconnaissance of holes, fractures,
the hollow stump of a pollard
seethes with earthy woodlice, beetles.

Head-down, fly-quick, alacritous,
the eye loses its whereabouts,
a shiver in the hedge, the wind
unsettles sailing butterflies.

# Primulas

Surprise again with their coloured rosettes,
blue primroses, the blue of a magpie's
feather, or the blue satin bowerbird,
are intermingled with purple, brick-red,
some hidden by Elizabethan ruffs,
all bearing warty flippered leaves,
oxlip and primrose crossed in their palettes,
here by a showery unleaved tree
in early March, with first courtship displays,
under the mahonia's prickly sprays,
two sparring bluetits, bright as primulas,
anticipating lilac-scented days.

# Black Tulips

Translated into white lilies,
the petals have a grapeskin's sheen
and corresponding purple-black,
each one's a glass of port, held high
in a collective toast, their silk's
a ruched Schiaparelli gown,
unflawed in its consistency,
its vintage concentration.
They're slow to open out or crack,
their own planetary formation
is tight, imperious, their caste
is of reassembled caesars,
each flaunting a purple toga
to their assassins. They'll be found,
blood-streaked, rain-beaten to the ground.

# Ipheion

Nectar-scented, garlicky
after rain, white petals blued finely
so that they seem composed of wind,
clear air-flowers, twinkly
gold vaults to the early bee,
tintings of transpicuous lavender
we find after a cloud tilt, and the ray
isolates more close-up, clearly.

A low lying discovery
for us hazarding scented showers,
your pink eye colours match the viburnum's
snowballs – and our new galaxy
of white stars are luminous now,
and what they are is closer to
something we can't remember, but once knew.

# The Passing

Wait out of night and listen to the rain;
your evocation of things time erased
won't clarify the present. A decade

becomes an epoch in the listening,
dust on the word, the time-film memorised
by you then no-one, so commemorate
its vanishing.

And after rain the light from star to star
suggesting high points – it was poetry
used up that silver, crowned the mirrored lake
with pink and white explosive nenuphar.

Bass-throbs of bubbling frogs, nearer jasmine;
they won't return, nor see the peach-red glow
of an inviting lamp, an open page

demanding words, nocturnal
signatures in berry-ink, elder-jet.
Wait under eaves for the green god to drum
an oak trunk, and the badger leave its sett.

# Forsythia and Snowflakes

A tilting lace filigree, rosette
in a blue hexagonal,
gauze mesh-sieve of igniting sparks,
powders as a solitary

visitant from the upper blue,
a moth holding equipoise
on a spray of shock yellow,
white dab of an eyelashed crystal,

making tangible components
of the atomic dance,
that find form in the freezing,
scintillae of a rainbow;

and is followed in succession
by a white cherry blossom
of flakes come to settle
on this yellow wind-bush.

Air-fires parachuting
as siftings of ash,
spectacular cobwebbings,
each jewel-pointed flash

is strung out like an orb web
on yellow trumpet shells,
a momentary star-map
from the nearer azure,

enquiring with its radial points
of its falling random here,
polyhedral pulsar
living on the temperature.

# Elder Wine

Timothy grass and cow parsley
silked by the wind; head cradled back
in verticals of green, I lay,
an insect supine on the track,

unable to regain balance,
carapace grained by jags of straw,
while over me a thistle flower
was kneaded by a kitten's paw –

a bluetit crammed its craw with seeds.
Lethargy of the white June day
saturated with elder flowers
mustily scented as red may,

its surf of colour faded to
bitty pinks of sweet william.
Coolness was the flagged wine-cellar,
wine fermentation, damson jam . . .

We picked white flowers for unguents,
creamy umbels with bitter leaves,
a recipe for complexion,
grass burs hung seed-spores on our sleeves,

and by midday, standing stirrup
on the farm hill we'd hear the tick
of the postman's unserviced bike,
no brakes, to hedge-crash was the trick . . .

Late summer saw our fingers mauve
from berrying, the violet pitch
of ripeness weighed the elders down,
rose-hips ripened by the ditch.

Commemorative with new bottles,
we drank last season's cool black wine,
watching how light restored to it,
returned the berry's purple shine.

# Clearance

Arrivals and departures: swallows gone,
a grey swathe of thistleheads floating free,
these days of mechanized farm rivalry
demand each year an earlier harvest,

devastation of hedgerows, ordered fields.
And we who've lacked the judicious foresight
to thin our lives of tree-climbing ivy,
search for the knife-blade we buried in bark,

too rusty now to show the vibrant edge
of the winning point thrown to find its mark.
Look how the years have uncovered dead roots,
time we thought the prerogative of youth

has undone what was fecund, left a field
so high in nettles, it's too late to hope
a path can be cleared to the other side.
Their raffishness commands the downward slope.

Sadly and early I walk out through lanes,
the autumn landscape's burnished, gold and pink.
Walking unravels memories, I find
my certain direction leads to the brink . . .

We stay together, but in deep mistrust,
the ciderish windfalls have turned to rot,
sloe-gin's no palliative, nor silence,
and yet we learn to live with what we've got.

# Hazel

Pre-empting spring, a straggled stool
of disparate branches, no trunk,
was alive with catkin-tassels,
a coppice of golden pendants,

each quivering like a wind-bell,
or here and there, spaced in hedgerows,
blasted by the wind, singular.
The road was bitter like our mood;

hill-sheep wouldn't budge for a car,
but formed small islands on the route
to the Quantocks; a stark beech wood
slammed to the testing of its roots,

and swirls of gold pollen pimpled
the roadside banks. We bit the cold,
our faces slapped hard by the wind,
testy, ears hidden by a hood,

our steps directed for Culbone,
Coleridge's farmhouse solitude,
the broody landscape of Ash Farm.
Two out together, but alone,

we walked with vengeance, faces set
into a needle rain of sleet,
grievances, recriminations,
vehemence issued at blood-heat,

and no protection anywhere,
inside or out, we turned around,
stamping back to the gold hazels,
besoms stood upright in the ground,

leafless, their crimson fibred buds
promising a rich autumn store
of nuts. We stood there, blood-deafened,
hearing the wind, the channel roar.

# Devil's Hole

The climb down was so tortuous,
each craggy jut, an overshoot
into the swell that boiled below,
the wiry seapink at one's foot,

was rooted half in earth, half air,
nature existing on the edge,
white campion, a claw of gorse.
We platformed on a shallow ledge,

the sea below us seemed to spin
with revolutions of a top,
a lurch taking the sky with it:
a seagull hung dead in that drop,

volplaning on the glassy air . . .
Fishing rods strapped to us, our slow
descent was to the Devil's Hole,
a cave gouged in the cliff below,

once used by smugglers, wreckers' lamps
spitting redly into the squall,
survivors butchered on this slab –
each head a bruised and battered ball,

were thrown back to the sea, offal
for crabs, or dragged in by the tide.
The sea blasted the rock. Once down,
our ritual was to browse inside,

turn over what the sea had flung
out of its throat, corroded spoil,
misshapen, sculpted by currents,
stones loosed after millennial toil,

things treasured in our secret crypt.
We came back to the light as two,
reborn, facing the sun, our eyes
planted widely into the blue,

and climbed around the coast to where,
mackerel were frisking for whitebait,
hearing the lighthouse bell, the surf
roar through the gulleys in a spate.

# Burnt Hemlock

Dried hemlock blackens to the residue
left by a fire, carpels in a crater,
they fracture underfoot, shiver and crack,

a burnt out field that met me shoulder high
was sticked, and where the speedwell's beady blue
poked through their roots, my eye was winning back

the afternoon I heard our neighbour's shout,
eyes raised to the red burning in the sky,
and to the molten debris blasted out

into the hemlock's white floating umbels.
A passenger aircraft was nosing down
above the dunes, and in our room a fly

was over-voluble, raspingly loud.
Weeks later, browsing through the waste places,
we raked out the segment of a helmet,

the handle of a case, a metal star,
small things, depersonalised, caught in the fret
of hemlock with its measled stems. I tread

through brittle dryness, a hollow bamboo-
grove, conscious of remains, there's something here
that won't stay down. The spider drops a thread . . .

# Eclipse

A slower resonance – it is the stone
answering the sun's vibrations,
and once you heard that central pulse in space,

a drum at the eclipse, and couldn't right
the alteration in you, nor balance
for knowledge of the earth's rotating cone,

but went off low and hid inside the bark
of a hollow oak, eyes closed in the dark.

# Thin Crust

My footsteps test each surface with the trained
   expertise of an attuned ear
finding the ring in crystal. Once attained,

the echo confirms trust, or has me halt,
   one foot raised like a cautious horse,
the ear and eye enquiring of the fault

in the way forward. Going back I find
   no confirmation of my trail,
no imprint on the crust, that left behind,

assures me of my passage. The remains
   of a wood-fire, a spitted fowl
have been erased, levelled out by the rains

that cancel history. Up on that hill,
   the last community's white flag
shows like a snow window, then hangs stock-still.

My movement's circular; they've come and gone,
   civilizations of a world,
leaving in the earth deposits of bone,

black blood, raised cities. I orbit no past,
   we here are too removed to read
our advancement in a genetic caste.

I move forward, exploratory, alone,
   crows flap into an azure sky.
I try for the resilience of stone,

something that's rooted. We are transient;
   the many went this way and lost.
I'm told history has its precedent.